Happy THE Ambitious

Welcoming God's Ambition for Us

Happy THE Ambitious

Welcoming God's Ambition for Us

By Thomas Joachim

Translated by Maria Kocisko

Scepter

Happy the Ambitious, by Thomas Joachim, is © 2024 by Scepter Publishers, Inc., a translation of the original French edition, *Heureux les ambitieux*, translated by Maria Kocisko. Original work is © 2022 by Editions des Beatitudes, Nouan le Fuzelier, France. This English language edition is published with permission from Editions des Beatitudes.

This English translation is published by Scepter Publishers, Inc.
Certain quotations have been stylistically adjusted to ensure consistency throughout the text.
info@scepterpublishers.org
www.scepterpublishers.org
800-322-8773
New York

Cover image: Jacob's Dream by Bartolome Esteban Murillo, Wikimedia Commons
Cover design by Rose Design
Page design and composition by Rose Design

ISBN paperback: 978-1-59417-546-6
ISBN eBook: 978-1-59417-547-3
Library of Congress Control Number: 2024952363

Printed in the United States of America

CONTENTS

PART THREE:
God's Seven Ambitions for Us / 63

INTRODUCTION

"I have such ambition for your soul."[1]

—St. Elizabeth of the Trinity

TO THE MAN WHO DARES not go on, Jesus says: "Friend, move up higher" (Lk 14:10). Maurice Zundel, a twentieth century Swiss theologian, suggests this understanding of Jesus' message: "Climb higher—the end will never be reached! Climb higher! You can only be fulfilled through the divine, you can only satisfy your desires by going all the way, even into infinity."[2] In this book we will consider exactly why and how to "go higher;" why and how to be ambitious.

It might seem contradictory to speak of ambition in a positive sense. Ambition has a bad reputation, especially among Catholics. It evokes pride, vanity, rivalry, and often ridicule. The etymology of the word itself doesn't help; the English word "ambition" comes from

1. Elizabeth of the Trinity, "Letter 270," in *Œuvres Complètes*, (Paris: Cerf, 2007), p. 676. Our translation.

2. Maurice Zundel, *Ta parole est comme une source* (Québec: Anne Sigier, 1967), p. 60. Our translation.

the Latin verb *ambire*, which means "to go around."[3] In the Middle Ages this referred to the rounds that political candidates would make in order to gain votes. Therefore, the word "ambition" carries the idea of wooing potential supporters, and with it every resulting implication of pushiness and baseness. What's more, ambition is only mentioned a few times in the Bible, and always in reference to sin.[4]

So why write a book about ambition? And why proclaim, "Happy are the Ambitious"? The answer is in the subtitle: we will consider "*God's* ambition for us." My intention is not to exalt worldly ambition, but rather to show how we can humbly cooperate with the vast desire God has for us.

---

3. See *Merriam Webster's Collegiate Dictionary*, 11th ed. (2019), s.v. "ambition."

4. Hebrew and Greek have no true biblical equivalent to the Latin *ambitio* (ambition) or *ambitiosus* (ambitious). These Latin words do, however, appear several times in the Vulgate as translations for pride, vanity, and pomp. (For example, 1 Cor 15:5; 2 Macc 4:7; Acts 25:23). The TOB (*Translation Œcuménique de la Bible)* uses "ambitious" [ambitieux] once to translate the Hebrew word *râhâv* (proud, puffed up) in Psalm 101:5: "a haughty look, an ambitious heart, I cannot endure." The word "ambition" does appear several times with a positive meaning in the Jerusalem Bible, however this is in translation of Greek words such as *philotimia* (love of honor), *zéloô* (burning with zeal), or *philotimeomai* (to be animated by love of honor). See Wis 14:18; 1 Cor 12:31; 1 Cor 14:1; 1 Cor 14:39; 2 Cor 5:9.

What if we better understood how great his ambition is for us? We would no doubt love life more, we would be energized, we would be more enthusiastic! That is the inspiration behind this book. We live in a dejected age. We sometimes call it the age of nothingness, of disenchantment, of nihilism, of the dissolution of values. In such a context, it is urgent that we rediscover the desire for greatness, attitudes of trust and confidence in life, and the energy to go forward. This is the attitude we see in children.

In the first part of this book, titled "Ambitious Like Children," I will try to show how striving for what is great characterizes the true childlike spirit we find in the Gospel. This will underline the positive character of ambition.

Secondly, I will explore how we can cooperate with divine ambition. In the section titled "Three Essential Elements of Ambition," I will emphasize those aspects of our interior life which must be developed if we are to enter into God's ambition for us: desire, confidence, and a fighting spirit.

I will present the third part, "God's Seven Ambitions for Us" as a commentary on the *Our Father.* This is where we will find the key to Christian ambition, for we can only live out God's desire for us by praying that he himself will accomplish it within us.

PART ONE

Ambitious Like Children

"All grown-ups were children first.
(But few of them remember it.)
So I correct my dedication:
To Leon Werth, when he was a little boy."[1]
—Antoine de Saint-Exupéry

WE MIGHT SAY THERE IS a "good" sort of ambition and a "bad" one. Both tend toward a certain greatness, but differ in their end and their means:

1. A "good ambition" envisions something truly magnificent, while a corrupt ambition envisions only a higher position, such as the ambition of a social climber who strives more for praise than true greatness.
2. A person with positive ambition behaves nobly, conscious of others, while the social climber uses

---

1. Antoine de Saint-Exupéry, dedication in *The Little Prince,* trans. Richard Howard (San Diego: Harcourt, 2000).

any means necessary to attain their goal and satisfy their narcissism.

In classical language, however, this distinction almost never appears. The word "ambition" has only recently gained a positive meaning, through the influence of liberalism which has used it as a driving force for action. For this reason, we must first consider the positive side of ambition: "A man is not unhappy because he has ambition, but because he is devoured by it."[2]

2. Charles de Montesquieu, *My Thoughts*, trans. Henry C. Clark (Indianapolis: Liberty Fund, 2012), no. 30.

1

A Little History of Magnanimity

"In a word, man knows that he is wretched.
He is therefore wretched, because he is so;
but he is really great because he knows it."[1]

—Pascal

THE ANCIENT GREEKS CREATED a word to express the ideal of greatness: magnanimity (*megalopsychia*).[2] According to their culture, this disposition of soul had a heroic aspect, often expressed in the refusal to accept an insult. We remember, for example, Achilles' response when his mother Thetis advised him that if he renounced pursuit of his enemy, he would live a long and happy life. If he sought vengeance, however, he

1. Blaise Pascal, *Penseés*, trans. W.F. Trotter (New York: Dutton, 1958), no. 416.

2. The English word comes more directly from the Latin *magnanimitas* (*magnus-anima*) which was used to translate the Greek *megalopsychia*. It literally means the "great soul" or "greatness of soul."

would die in battle. Achilles responded proudly, "So I as well, if a like fate be set for me, shall lie when I shall fall. But now may I gain a noble glory. . . ."[3]

The Greeks also understood another, more philosophical greatness of soul: to be impassive in the face of life's trials. Take, for example, Socrates who was given a cup of poison to drink as a sentence of execution. He drank it calmly in one go, while continuing to philosophize (on the idea of death) with his disciples.[4]

When Christianity encountered Greek and Roman thought, magnanimity was not immediately adopted as a Christian virtue. It seemed lofty and proud. Christians did not trust this appetite for greatness which looked like pride, and did not understand how it could harmonize with Christian humility. Not only did the word "magnanimity" (*megalopsychia)* not appear in the Greek translation of the Bible, but the image of Jesus on the Cross was nothing like the stoic Socrates. So much so, in fact, that the pagans mocked him for it: "what a pitiful spectacle he is, how far from the impassive serenity of the wise man! He trembles in the face of suffering. He is afraid; he says nothing before the

3. See Homer, *The Iliad*, trans. Alston Hurd Chase and William G. Perry Jr. (Boston: Little, Brown & Co, 1950), bk. 18, p. 331.

4. See Plato, *Phaedo.*

judge; at the climax he cries out for help; No—he is not strong, but weak."[5]

We can thank St. Thomas Aquinas, in the thirteenth century, for showing how magnanimity can be compatible with humility, how we can consider ourselves worthy of recognition while also acknowledging that we owe it all to God.[6] According to him, these two attitudes are intertwined—there is no magnanimity without humility, and no humility without magnanimity. How can this be? Because in man we find both grandeur and wretchedness, all at once. As Pascal said, man in his nature is, "A Nothing in comparison with the Infinite, an All in comparison with the Nothing, a mean between nothing and everything."[7] Man can therefore be magnanimous, when he considers the dignity and talents he has received from God, and also judge himself as little, when he considers his shortcomings. Far from contradicting one another, magnanimity and humility balance each other out.[8] Without

---

5. Cited by Origen in *Contra Celsum,* 7, 53, ed. Koetschau (Leipzig, 1899), vol. 2, p. 203.

6. See Aquinas, *Summa Theologica*, trans. Fathers of the English Dominican Province, Second Revised Edition (Canton, OH: Pinnacle Press, 2017), 2-2.129. See especially article 3.

7. Pascal, *Penseés*, no. 72.

8. See Aquinas, *Summa Theologica*, 2-2.129.3-4.

the sense of greatness of soul, humility becomes a psychological regression; without humility, magnanimity is mere presumption.

In the seventeenth century, magnanimity and humility began again to be disassociated, and the desire for greatness was sought after largely outside of Christian ideals. The Modernists progressively substituted magnanimity with the notion of "generosity" or the "will to power." We know how fiercely Nietzsche adopted this attitude, setting it against humility and compassion, both of which horrified him. He considered humility to be a slave's virtue, despised by those of the "ruling group" who are "exalted [and] proud."[9] "Pity stands opposed to the tonic emotions which heighten our vitality: it has a depressing effect. We are deprived of strength when we feel pity."[10]

Today we still find this "will to power" in many self-help books, albeit in a sugarcoated way. We see it clearly in how "power" is used in the titles of many recent best-sellers, such as: *Unlimited Power* (Tony Robbins), *The Power of Intention* (Wayne Dyer), *The*

---

9. See Friedrich Nietzsche, *Beyond Good and Evil*, trans. Walter Kaufmann (Vintage Books: New York, 1989), no. 260. See also *The Twilight of Idols*, no. 31.

10. Friedrich Nietzsche, "The Antichrist" found in *The Portable Nietzsche*, trans. Walter Kaufmann (New York: Penguin Books, 1976), § 7.

Power of your Subconscious Mind (Joseph Murphy), *The Power of Now* (Eckhart Tolle), and so on. These works undeniably arouse a desire for greatness. The subtitle of *The Magic of Thinking Big* (David Schwartz, 1953), one of the first best-sellers of the genre, is indicative of this: "Acquire the secrets of success . . . Achieve everything you've always wanted!" In his book, David Schwartz hammers home the point, at length, that we must *think big* in order to make great things happen in our lives. To get there, we must make a habit of positive thinking, anticipating our success. The ancient world's greatness of soul is here transformed into "positive thinking," with this seemingly magical idea that if we keep visualizing success, we will eventually get it.

These days, the word "magnanimity" seems a bit outdated; it has been all but forgotten. For this reason, I will refer instead to ambition throughout this book, but with the clarification that ambition is more of a passion than a virtue.[11] This is why there can be "good" and "bad" ambition, but there can never be bad virtue, or bad magnanimity.

---

11. A virtue is a disposition—acquired in a permanent way—that inclines us toward doing good, whereas a passion is a feeling which animates us, an emotion which can push us equally toward doing good or evil. Consider anger, for example. Anger can push us to work for justice, but can also drive us to unjust violence. Virtue, however, the opposite of vice, always leads us to good.

2

Bad Ambition

"Love is not ambitious."[1]

—Saint Paul

AS WE HAVE DISCUSSED, bad ambition seeks worldly precedence rather than greatness. As Cicero said (and he knew very well of what he spoke), "the more notable a man is for his greatness of spirit, the more ambitious he is to be the foremost citizen, or I should say rather, to be sole ruler."[2] The following chapter will consider the three main negative aspects of this disordered desire for superiority: in terms of ourselves, in terms of others, and in terms of God. This will also help us to see in contrast, and better understand, the triple-benefit of good ambition.

1. 1 Cor 13:5. Translated by the author from the Vulgate, which uses the Latin word *ambitiosa* to translate the Greek *askèmonei,* referring to dishonorable, dishonest action. Certain translations, notably the French Vigouroux translation, also translate it in this way.

2. Cicero, *De Officiis*, trans. Walter Miller, Loeb Classical Library (London: William Heinemann, 1928) ch. 19, no. 64.

1. Ambition Can Be Vain and Toxic for Us

The Merriam-Webster Dictionary defines ambition as "an ardent desire for rank, fame, or power."[3] St. Thomas Aquinas said that "ambition signifies inordinate love of honor"[4] and Spinoza that "ambition is the immoderate desire of glory."[5] Let us examine how this excess of narcissism can be both vain and toxic.

To start with, ambition is vain. We say of the devil that the more he has, the more he desires. The same can be said of an ambitious person. They are always unsatisfied, insatiable. The more recognition they receive, the more they desire, as though haunted by an infinite incompleteness. The great drama of the ambitious person is their greed, always lacking *just a little more* glory. They will always be more dissatisfied with what they don't have, than content with what they do have.[6] Never satisfied, the ambitious person will never finish being ambitious.

---

3. *Merriam-Webster's Dictionary*, s.v. "ambition."

4. Aquinas, *Summa Theologica*, 2-2.131.2.

5. Benedict de Spinoza, "Ethics," in *Great Books of the Western World*, ed. Robert Maynard Hutchins, vol. 31 (Chicago, IL: Encyclopaedia Britannica, 1952), third part, prop. 59, no. 44.

6. See François Fénelon: "Avarice and ambition are more displeased with what they lack than they are satisfied with what they possess." (*Pensées et Maximes recueillies par M. Duval*, ed. Rolland (Paris, 1821).

Ambition is dangerous as well as vain. Great gains often come before great falls! The ancient Romans had a saying: *Arx tarpeia Capitoli proxima* ("The Tarpeian Rock is close to the Capitol"). It meant that one falls quickly from glory (signified by the Capitol, where the Temple of Jupiter stood) to degradation (signified by the Tarpeian Rock, situated right by the Temple, from which condemned men were thrown to their deaths). The more we dream of grandeur, the greater the fall will be. . . .

Bad ambition also often leads to dishonesty. The ambitious man, driven by his desire to be applauded, no longer discerns the means he takes to achieve his end. He may desire recognition for a quality he does not necessarily possess, and to get it he may turn to conniving, lying, or taking drugs. Salluste, a Roman historian of the first century BC, remarked upon this well before major sporting competitions such as the Tour de France: ". . . the noble and the base alike long for glory, honor, and power, but the former mount by the true path, whereas the latter, being destitute of noble qualities, rely upon craft and deception."[7]

---

7. Salluste, *The War with Catiline*, trans. J. C. Rolfe, Loeb Classical Library, (London: Heinemann, 1921), ch. 11, p. 37.

It's not that the ambitious man is completely incapable of achieving his goals (unlike the presumptuous man), but by seeking glory above all else he can easily become a liar in order to achieve his end.

2. Ambition Can Be Toxic for Others

Just as love of money can lead to all sorts of maliciousness and crime,[8] ambition can often lead to hurting others. Not only does the ambitious man hoard his prestige as the miser hoards his money—doing nothing good with it for others—but he will also be ready to do anything to take the place of someone in his way. "Get out of there, so I can take your place!" Jean-Louis Bruguès has good reason to say that "ambition constitutes an intense egoism."[9] The ambitious man objectifies others, manipulates, reduces them either to obstacles or means to attain his end. Kant condemned ambition as "a vice opposed to the respect which every man can rightfully claim."[10]

---

8. See 1 Tim 6:10: "For the love of money is the root of all evils. . . ."

9. Jean-Louis Bruguès, *Dictionnaire de Morale Catholique*, (Chambray: CLD, 1991), p. 31.

10. Immanuel Kant, "The Doctrine of Virtue," part 2 of *The Metaphysics of Morals,* trans. Mary J. Gregor (New York: Harper & Row), § 42.

3. Ambition May Oppose God's Glory

Harmful ambition is not only toxic for us and others, but it can stand in opposition to God's own glory. The ambitious man easily attributes all his merits to himself, rather than offering them back to God. When St. Paul asks, "What have you that you did not receive?"[11] he would gladly reply, "Everything!" As Bossuet rightly saw, concealed in ambition is a desire to be divine: "What flatters the ambitious is the idea of omnipotence, which seems to make gods of them on earth."[12] The Church of Laodicea in the Book of Revelation is an exact picture of this state of soul. God speaks to it in reproof: "For you say, I am rich, I have prospered, and I need nothing; not knowing that you are wretched, pitiable, poor, blind, and naked" (Rv 3:17).

To summarize what we have described as "bad ambition," we might consider the story of Abimelech (See Jgs 6–9). He was the first king in the history of Israel, and he plotted his way to the throne, even though no prophet had called upon him to reign. In his desire for power, he killed his seventy half-brothers (besides

11. 1 Cor 4:7.

12. Bossuet, *Politics Drawn From the Very Words of Holy Scripture* (New York: Cambridge University Press, 1990), p. 381.

Yotam, who had hidden himself away). However, Abimelech came to a lamentable end—as he attempted to burn down the town of Thebets, an unnamed woman threw a millstone onto his head. He who sought to elevate himself was struck down by a rock that seemed to come from heaven; he who dreamt of glory was grotesquely killed.

3

Good Ambition

"How happy is a life that begins with love
and ends with ambition!
If I had to choose, this is the one I should take."[1]

—Pascal

WE HAVE SEEN HOW THE QUEST for grandeur can be harmful, for ourselves, others, and the glory of God. Now we will look, conversely, at how good ambition can be an amazing energizer, and how it can serve the good of others, all oriented toward God's glory.

1. Good Ambition is Beneficial for Us

One of the good things about ambition is that it gets us out of our comfort zone and motivates us to action. It's a revitalizing passion, a desire full of hope and audacity.

---

1. Blaise Pascal, "Discourse on the Passion of Love," in *The Harvard Classics Volume 48, Blaise Pascal: Thoughts, Letters & Minor Works,* ed. Charles W. Eliot (New York: P.F. Collier & Son, 1910), p. 418.

A well-oriented ambition brings out the best in us; the sense of greatness brings out our talents. Ambition is a great reservoir of energy that can propel us onward, toward the good. As Hegel famously put it, "Nothing great in the world has been accomplished without passion."[2] To this point, we cannot forget that Jesus did not say, "Blessed are the weak," but, "Blessed are the meek!" We must be strong to be truly meek; or else we are simply passive, amorphous. We must have determination before we can be flexible, otherwise we are just indecisive. We must be ambitious before we can get underway: "Great ambitions make for great things."[3]

2. Good Ambition Serves Others

God gives us the talents which allow us to excel in certain areas, with the intention that all might benefit from them. In this way, we are connected to one another. Every gift from God is destined for the good of all. When Mother Teresa received the Nobel Peace Prize, it is unlikely she accepted it for love of

2. Georg Wilhelm Friedrich Hegel, *Philosophy of History*, found in *Great Books of the Western World*, ed. Robert Maynard Hutchins, vol. 46 (Chicago: Encyclopedia Britannica, 1952), p. 163.

3. Victor Hugo, *Littérature et philosophie mêlées* (Paris: Albin Michel, 1934) p. 7. Our translation.

honor—worthy though she may have been to receive it—but rather because it was a means to promote service to the poor. As Bossuet said, "The greatness which is given one—far from weakening their goodness—is only given to help them give more of themselves, like a fountain elevated to pour forth upon all."[4]

Solomon's prayer in Psalm 72 illustrates this well. At first glance it seems improper and prideful:

> Give the king thy justice, O God . . . May he have dominion from sea to sea, and from the River to the ends of the earth. May his foes bow down before him, and his enemies lick the dust . . . May all kings fall down before him, all nations serve him. . . . (1, 8–9, 11)

To pray in this way, asking for greater fame, greater power, greater popularity, seems to completely miss the point! However, continued reading brings us to a better understanding of King Solomon's intention. If he asks for an extension of his influence, he does so in order to care for the weak:

> May he defend the cause of the poor of the people, give deliverance to the needy, and crush the

4. Jacques-Bénigne Bossuet, "Oraison funèbre de Louis de Bourbon," in *Œuvres* (Paris: Gallimard, 1970), p. 200. Our translation.

> oppressor . . . For he delivers the needy when he calls, the poor and him who has no helper. He has pity on the weak and the needy, and saves the lives of the needy. From oppression and violence he redeems their life; and precious is their blood in his sight. (4, 12–14)

The ambition which conforms to God's heart seeks not to exalt the self, nor to dominate the other, but to be able to help the one who is most in need.

3. Ambition for God

Ambition is also a powerful force that can orient us toward God and away from evil. Ambition pushes us to "grow up in every way into him who is the head, into Christ" (Eph 4:15). If the only gain we strive for is the love of Jesus, then desiring greatness is desiring to glorify God with our whole lives. This is the kind of ambition we see when St. Elizabeth of the Trinity writes "My one ambition is to be Love's victim,"[5] or when St. Thérèse of the Child Jesus says that she has no other ambition than to be "little Jesus' donkey"[6] and to make

---

5. Elizabeth of the Trinity, *The Praise of Glory*, trans. The Benedictines of Stanbrook (New York: Braunfell Books, 2022), pp. 129–130.

6. Thérèse of Lisieux, "Letter 204," *Œuvres Complètes* (Paris: Cerf et DDB, 1992), p. 564. Our translation.

him "known and loved."[7] While worldly ambition seeks honor and ephemeral splendor, the saints "are ambitious for nobler riches."[8] They live their lives *Ad maiorem Dei gloriam*, "for the greater glory of God."[9]

The ambitious man, if he wishes to remain good, will keep two simple things in mind: first, that he has received his talents from God, and that he has received them for the service of others and to glorify God with his life.

---

7. Thérèse of Lisieux, "Prayer 8," *Œuvres Complètes* (Paris: Cerf et DDB, 1992), p. 966. Our translation.

8. Louis Racine, *Religion, A Poem* (Paris: 1742), chant 3, p. 100.

9. This saying by Gregory the Great was used several times by Ignatius of Loyola, and so it became the Jesuit motto.

4

The Spirit of Childhood

"We have Christ as an infant; let us grow up with him."[1]

—St. Augustine

One day, while Jesus' disciples were arguing about who was the greatest among them, Jesus placed a child in their midst and said to them, "Truly, I say to you, unless you turn and become like children, you will never enter the kingdom of heaven" (Mt 18:3). By putting a child among the Twelve, Jesus put that child in the midst of the Church, as though to say, "Take a good look at this child, place him at the center of your community, for he exemplifies your vocation."

But what is a child? What truly characterizes a child? We might say, for example, that children are trusting, open, innocent, and pure. This is all true. But what most characterizes a child is that they want to be

1. Augustine, "Sermon 196, On Christmas Day," in *The Works of St. Augustine, Part 3: Sermons* (New Rochelle, NY: New City Press, 1993), p. 62.

big. They never stop talking about it—"When I grow up, this . . . when I grow up, that. . . ." The child is ambitious, in a positive sense. Hegel understood this and highlighted a feeling particular to children—that of dissatisfaction with being the way they are. He writes of their "desire to belong to the adult world whose superiority they divine, [and] the longing to grow up."[2] Having said this, what most opposes the spirit of childhood is not ambition, but "Peter Pan Syndrome." We must understand this if we are to stop putting ambition at odds with a childlike spirit, putting magnanimity at odds with humility.

1. Peter Pan Syndrome

The story of Peter Pan, "the boy who wouldn't grow up,"[3] was made into an amusing animated movie by Walt Disney, but the story behind the novel which inspired it is much less joyful.[4] We remember the story: Peter Pan is a little boy who refuses to grow up, and

2. G.W.F. Hegel, "Philosophy of Right," in *Great Books of the Western World*, ed. Mortimer J. Adler, vol. 46 (Chicago IL: Enclyclopaedia Britannica, 1952) no. 175, p. 61.

3. James-Matthew Barrie told the story of Peter Pan in several different versions, one of which was a play titled *Peter Pan, or The Boy Who Wouldn't Grow Up* (1904).

4. On this subject, see Kathleen Kelly-Lainé, *Peter Pan: The Story of a Lost Childhood* (Rockville, MD: Element Books, 1997).

who persuades Wendy to follow him to the imaginary "Never Never Land" where they have extraordinary adventures as they are pursued by Captain Hook. During their adventures, Wendy and Peter promise each other to never grow up. However, years later, Peter finds Wendy Darling again, and she explains to him that she has long since grown up, that she couldn't help it, and that she has even become a mother. Peter then falls to the ground and bursts into tears. . . .

The author of this story, James-Matthew Barrie, tragically lost his brother David when David was thirteen years old. James, aged six, did everything he could to console his mother, and even tried dressing up in his deceased brother's clothes. But his mother was inconsolable. Some psychoanalysts believe that J.M. Barrie therefore held on to the idea that growing up was a bad thing. This is what has been termed "Peter Pan Syndrome"—anguish about growing up, leaving childhood behind, becoming an adult.[5]

If we think about it, Peter Pan contradicts the spirit of childhood. As theologian Karl Barth noted:

> He who wants to be a child is not a child; he is merely childish. He who is a child does not want to be a

---

5. Refer, for example, to Dan Kiley's, *The Peter Pan Syndrome: Men Who Have Never Grown Up* (New York: Avon Books, 1983).

child; he takes his play, his study, his first attempts at accomplishment, his first wrestlings with his environment, in bitter earnest, as though he were already an adult. In so doing he is genuinely childlike.[6]

2. The Inferiority Complex and the Will to Power

In his desire to be great, the child can also prove to be tyrannical: barely born, he aspires to the empire![7] The psychoanalyst Alfred Adler developed an entire theory on this subject in his writings on the "inferiority complex" connected with the desire to grow up. According to him, the child first harbors an inferiority complex which, stimulated by the will to power, is transformed into the aspiration to growth.[8] The beginning of our psychological existence is marked by a feeling of inferiority, which is offset by the desire to be great, or even

6. Karl Barth, *Church Dogmatics*, vol. 3, part 4 (Edinburgh: T. & T. Clark, 1961), §56, 2, p. 609.

7. This idea, belonging to Rousseau, and its contrast with the story of Peter Pan are developed by Éric Deschavanne and Pierre-Henri Tavoillot in *Philosophie des âges de la vie*. Rousseau resolved this problem for himself by placing his five children in an orphanage, which gave him a more peaceful environment to write his treatise on education!

8. For a study of the inferiority complex according to Alfred Adler, see chapter 6 of his book, *Le Sens da la vie, étude de psychologie individuelle*, trans. Herbert Schaffer (Paris: Éditions Payot, 1968).

to be the greatest. The feeling of inadequacy somehow becomes the fuel for our success.

When we were "little," we might not have coped well with being smaller than almost everybody else! It is also possible that, far from discouraging us, this feeling of inferiority motivated us. Let us, however, acknowledge that the child's appetite for grandeur is not perfect. In the same way that there can be a good ambition and a bad one, there can also be a childlike spirit which is worthy of the Gospel, or one that is more "Nietzschean!"

3. Nietzsche and St. Thérèse of the Child Jesus

Regarding childhood and greatness, the two most contradictory figures of the late nineteenth century are probably Friedrich Nietzsche and St. Thérèse of the Child Jesus. Everything about them seems in opposition to the other. While one declared himself to be "one of Christianity's most terrible adversaries,"[9] the other was considered by Pope Pius X to be "the greatest saint of modern times." St. John Paul II even proclaimed her to be a Doctor of the Church. However, these two characters did both shine a light on the child's desire for greatness.

---

9. In a letter to Köselitz, dated November 13, 1888. Friedrich Nietzche, *Kritische Studienausgabe*, ed. G. Colli and M. Montinari, vol. 8 (München: de Gruyter, 2003), p. 467. Our translation.

The theme of childhood is the common thread in Nietzsche's major work, *Thus Spoke Zarathustra*. In it, Nietzsche imagines how Zarathustra, the presumed founder of the morality of good and evil, transforms himself into a child, in the sense that the child does not yet know the difference between good and evil. For Nietzsche, the "child" Zarathustra invites humanity to liberate itself from the idols of good and evil, in order to finally assume its full potential, to go from mere "human" to "superhuman." He illustrates a will to power which longs to be purely self-referential, refusing all culpability. A "will to power" that becomes a "will to always more power."

Even though St. Thérèse of the Child Jesus is naturally found in opposition to this vision, she also shows how the child aspires to greatness, and to a life lived beyond guilt:

> Yes, I feel it; even though I had on my conscience all the sins that can be committed, I would go, my heart broken with sorrow, and throw myself into Jesus' arms, for I know how much he loves the prodigal child who returns to him.[10]

---

10. Thérèse of Lisieux, *Story of a Soul*, trans. John Clarke, O.C.D. (Washington, DC: ICS Publications, 1996), Manuscript C, p. 259.

Here, the child surpasses guilt by raising herself to the height of divine mercy, and not by exalting herself. This is what is so different to Nietzsche's perspective, and Adler's. Rather, here we return to St. Thomas Aquinas' intuition, that we can aspire both to grandeur and humility all at once. Nothing could be clearer in this passage from *Story of a Soul*:

> I have always wanted to be a saint. Alas! I have always noticed that when I compared myself to the saints, there is between them and me the same difference that exists between a mountain whose summit is lost in the clouds and the obscure grain of sand trampled underfoot by passers-by. Instead of becoming discouraged, I said to myself: God cannot inspire unrealizable desires. I can, then, in spite of my littleness, aspire to holiness.[11]

Children can make a synthesis of the desire for greatness, a sense of helplessness, and hope. They aspire to great things (magnanimity), but sense their helplessness (humility), and so they can only rely on the greatness of another to reach the heights to which they aspire (hope). This is why the childlike spirit is the very spirit of Christianity. We are called to live

11. Thérèse of Lisieux, *Story of a Soul*, p. 207.

God's own life, but as we are only small creatures—and sinners, moreover—this is impossible for us. Our only option is to rely on God's grace to carry out our heavenly vocation.

4. Young at Heart

Ambition is a passion of the young. We speak more often of the ambitions of youth than those of old age. A certain ambitious tendency of older generations (regarding the preservation of power and money, and concern for their posterity) has something sad about it. However, ambition is not reserved for the young. Good ambition keeps us young for our whole lives! This passage from Samuel Ullman, made famous by General Douglas MacArthur, is worth citing in its entirety:

> Youth is not a time of life; it is a state of mind; it is not a matter of rosy cheeks, red lips and supple knees; it is a matter of the will, a quality of the imagination, a vigor of the emotions; it is the freshness of the deep springs of life.
>
> Youth means a temperamental predominance of courage over timidity of the appetite, for adventure over the love of ease. This often exists in a man of sixty more than a boy of twenty. Nobody grows

> old merely by a number of years. We grow old by deserting our ideals.
>
> Years may wrinkle the skin, but to give up enthusiasm wrinkles the soul. Worry, fear, self-distrust bows the heart and turns the spirit back to dust.
>
> Whether sixty or sixteen, there is in every human being's heart the lure of wonder, the unfailing child-like appetite of what's next, and the joy of the game of living. In the center of your heart and my heart there is a wireless station; so long as it receives messages of beauty, hope, cheer, courage and power from men and from the Infinite, so long are you young.
>
> When the aerials are down, and your spirit is covered with snows of cynicism and ice of pessimism, then you are grown old, even at twenty, but as long as your aerials are up, to catch the waves of optimism, there is hope you may die young at eighty.[12]

But how can we do it? To avoid the disillusionment that comes with youthful ambition, we must reverse the usual perspective of our life. We can no longer seek

12. Margaret E. Armbrester, *Samuel Ullman and "Youth": The Life, the Legacy* (Tuscaloosa, AL: University of Alabama Press, 2009).

to fulfill *our* ambitions; we must seek to welcome God's ambitions for us. Fulfilling our own dreams is not of primary importance, but rather that God's dreams for us are made real in our lives. So, what is this ambition God has for us?

The church fathers tell us that if God became man, it was so that man could become God. What greater thing could we imagine? God's ambition for us is to raise us up to himself. In God's eyes, nothing can be great enough for us until we resemble God's own self.

There are many things to say regarding the divinization of man. Certain spiritualities, inspired by those of the East, offer a false vision of divinization. They often involve a dilution of our "I am" in the infinite of the divine "I Am." And yet, this is impossible, since God's essence is uncreated, while our essence is created. This distinction between God and us is essential. We cannot become one being with him. However, we can become united to him through grace. This is the crucial point—it is by grace, and only by grace, that we can grow toward all that he calls us to.

This growth takes place in three distinct stages:

1. First, there is the moment when God creates our soul. We have all passed from nothingness into being, from non-existence to the marvel that

we are. Our conception represents a first step in divinization because, from the beginning, God created us in his image.

2. Next, there is the passage from nature to grace, notably through baptism. From that point on, we are not just created in God's image, but we participate in his divine life.[13]
3. Finally comes the passage from grace to glory, from earth to heaven, where "we shall be like him, for we shall see him as he is" (1 Jn 3:2).

The first stage is done; we cannot change one iota of it. The second stage is where we are at now, if we have already been baptized and are living in God's grace. The third stage is yet to come; this is the stage which defines the meaning of our life on earth: the passage from grace into glory.

---

13. See 2 Pt 1:3–4: "His divine power has granted to us all things that pertain to life and godliness, through the knowledge of him who called us to his own glory and excellence, by which he has granted to us his precious and very great promises, that through these you may . . . become partakers of the divine nature." In commentary on these verses, Thomas Aquinas specifies that divine nature, although not communicable in itself, can be communicated "according to the participation of some similitude (*secundum similitudinis participationem*)." For an interesting precision on the meaning of this passage, see Aquinas, *Summa Theologica*, 1.13.9-1.

We exist in a state of potential, from our conception to our death. We must transition from potential to action, from image to perfect resemblance (as perfect as possible!). This is God's ambition for us. Now we will consider the three qualities of soul that we must develop if we wish to cooperate with his design of love and its fulfillment.

PART TWO

Three Essential Elements of Ambition

"Hope in God!"

—Ps 42:11

NOW, LET US CONSIDER which attitudes are necessary for our ambition to become reality. How can we cooperate with God's ambition for us? How can we go from dreaming to action?

It can be a good thing to daydream, but we must find ways to act on our dreams so that they don't go up in smoke—or become nightmares. As Ernst Bloch said in *The Principle of Hope*, "Nobody has ever lived without daydreams, but it is a question of knowing them deeper and deeper and in this way keeping them trained unerringly, usefully, on what is right."[1] Therefore, in this second part we will consider how to keep

1. Ernst Bloch, *The Principle of Hope*, vol. 1, trans. Neville Plaice, Stephen Plaice, and Paul Knight, (Cambridge, MA: The MIT Press, 1986), p. 3.

our dreams "trained on what is right," by focusing on the three interior attitudes we must develop in order to have realistic ambitions: desire, confidence, and a fighting spirit.

Ambition is about attaining the object of our dreams; therefore, we must first cultivate the *desire* for our objective. We must also have *confidence* in our success, so that the desire does not fall into despair. Finally, we must have a *fighting spirit*, because great desires are rarely accomplished without effort. Desire, confidence, and a fighting spirit—these are the three essential attitudes for cooperating with God's ambition for us.

5

The Path of Desire

"The whole life of a good Christian is a holy desire . . . This is our life, that by longing we should be exercised."[1]

—St. Augustine

Benoît Garceau wrote a very good little book titled *La voie du désir*, or "The Path of Desire."[2] In it, he develops the idea that we are beings of desire, and that the best spirituality consists of deepening this desire into infinity. According to him, there are three main paths of dedication: those of obligation, need, and desire.

1. The dedication of obligation is distrustful of desire, instead placing greater value on faithfulness to the principles of life that we have given

1. Augustine, "Homily Four on the First Epistle of John" in *Nicene and Post-Nicene Fathers, First Series*, vol. 7, ed. Philip Schaff, (Buffalo, NY: Christian Literature Publishing, 1888), no. 6.

2. Benoît Garceau, *La voie du désir*, (Montreal: Médiaspaul, 1997), pp. 7–16. Our translation.

ourselves. This spirituality of "you must" is very noble, but often stifling.

2. The dedication of need is the exact opposite. It draws out the deep desire of our being and leads it to all-out consumption, according to the impulse of the moment. This dedication appears attractive at first, but leaves us immature and narcissistic, rather than guiding us toward wisdom.
3. The true dedication, that of desire, consists of "living in faithfulness to the deepest aspiration of our being," which is to love more and more.[3]

Our natural way of being ambitious is by dreaming of power. Our will to power is never satisfied; by its very nature it is the will to always more power. It confuses the world here and now, ruled by the law of whoever is strongest, with the world to come, ruled by goodness. It transforms the worship of performance into religion.

The correct path consists of receiving God's ambition for us and entering into his desire, rather than forging immense desires for ourselves based on our ego. It is about orienting our life toward God.

---

3. Benoît Garceau, *La voie du désir*, p. 16.

1. Putting Desire into Practice

For our dreams to become concrete and take shape, we must know what they will mean for tomorrow and the next day! We must go from vague inspiration to tangible plans. It's not enough to know "what" our ambition is, we must also figure out the "why" and the "how." Why do I have this ambition? What do I really want, deep down? What am I going to do in order to make it happen, and what do I need to get there?

These questions derive from prudence, the virtue that St. Augustine defined as "a love which chooses with wisdom."[4] Prudence first requires a "love," a desire, an end we seek. But it also requires us to choose a path to get there that is discerning and shrewd, perceiving exactly the right way forward given the circumstances. To achieve his ambition, the prudent man will begin by clarifying his intention and choosing the right way to go about it, given the current circumstances.

---

4. Augustine, quoted by J-L Brugès in *Dictionnaire de morale catholique* (Chambray: Éditions CLD, 1991), p. 346. The author did not give the reference. It could be an approximate translation from *De Moribus Catholicae Ecclesiae*, II, 1, § 15–25: *prudentia, amor ea quibus adjudatur ab eis quibus impeditur, sagiter seligens* ("prudence is love distinguishing with sagacity between what hinders it and what helps it").

From Desire to Intention

Most models of personal development begin with a suggested goal. They often speak of a vision. In the evangelical Christian world, this verse from Proverbs is often cited: "Where there is no prophesy the people cast off restraint" (Prv 29:18). This is true—without a broad vision, we work just one day at a time and the results are mediocre. To make our great ambitions a reality, we must first answer certain questions concerning the "target" of our action: What do we really want? What do we want to do, what do we want to experience, what do we want to be? In short—what are our main objectives? What is our priority? For what and for whom will I expend my energy? These questions are vital; if our life has no firm intention, we will be easily distracted from our goal. Without intention, our desires will remain daydreams. We will be like the foolish traveler that St. Gregory the Great speaks of, "who sees pleasant meadows on his journey and forgets where he is going."[5]

5. Gregory the Great, "Homily 15: I am the good shepherd" in *Forty Gospel Homilies*, trans. Dom David Hurst (Kalamazoo, MI: Cistercian Publications, 1990), p. 112.

From Intention to Action

If our ambition remains a dream, we will remain far from success, and it will disappear like smoke. Finding the "why" helps to motivate us, but answering "how" will make things doable.[6]

Before launching blindly into our project, we must be realistic about our potential: what are likely outcomes, and what is more risky? We each have strengths and weaknesses, and external circumstances make for both opportunities and threats. We must first make an inventory of these things so we can properly evaluate our situation.[7] Without a thorough evaluation, we will take random shots and most likely miss our target.

Here, by way of example, are several important questions we can ask ourselves:

1. *Strengths:* What can I rely on to succeed? What are my talents, my strengths? What am I good at doing, what do I like to do, and what do I want to continue doing? What do others consider to be my predominant quality?

---

6. On this point, see Simon Sinek's *Start With Why* (New York: Portfolio Publishing, 2009). See chapter eight in particular.

7. Here I will use the SWOT Analysis, which is well-known in the management world. SWOT stands for Strength, Weakness, Opportunity, Threat.

2. *Weaknesses:* What am I less capable, and what do I dislike doing? What are my limits, both objective and subjective? What do others consider to be my weak points? In what area do I need to grow?
3. *Opportunities:* Are there any positive, external circumstances that I can potentially draw on? Is there an open door, a good moment for action?
4. *Threats:* What are the foreseeable problems? Are these difficulties surmountable or not? What is the financial situation, for example? Are the logistics likely to go according to plan, or should I anticipate disaster? How can I be attentive and stay in control of any potential threats?

Once we have decided how to proceed given the circumstances, we must stop deliberating and act. If not, we might deliberate forever. Now comes the planning phase of the project, when we make things even more concrete. For example, there is a difference between deciding to "lose weight" (a vague idea) and deciding to lose ten pounds in five months, at a rate of two pounds a month (a concrete plan). To go from a vague idea to a concrete plan, we must ask ourselves "when" and "how." When will we know that we have reached our goal, and how will we measure it? What will our deadlines be as we reach this goal, in the long, medium, and short terms? And what does all this mean for tomorrow? In other words, what is the next step to take? Even a journey of one thousand miles begins with one little step . . . in the right direction.

2. God's Dream in Man's Dream

We often say that if we want to make God laugh, we should tell him our plans. This joke has some food for thought. Are our human plans trifling in the sight of divine governance? Do our ambitions seem ridiculous compared to God's ambition for us? Doesn't life itself prove this to us, taking us by surprise again and again? Timothy Radcliffe cites a sermon on this point, given at a solemn profession by a Scottish Dominican Provincial:

> I am coming to the end of my religious life and you are now beginning yours. As I look back over my religious life, and it has been a long one, I think of all that I have labored to build and to support. Often I have labored hard to construct something, to leave some monument behind me, when, inevitably, some idiot has come along after me and torn down all that I have built and called it progress. So, I want to give you this piece of counsel, whatever schemes you may hatch, whatever plans

> you may formulate, be sure of one thing, God will frustrate them![8]

We can certainly dream and make our plans, but we must remember that with God there is always a dream within the dream—even a dream within the dream of a dream! In a poem published in 1827, Edgar Allan Poe asked: "Is all that we see or seem / But a dream within a dream?"[9] Our little, budding dreams have something vain and trivial about them, but they are an opportunity for God to bring his own dreams to fulfillment through us.

Let us consider the Biblical story of Tobit. In this wonderful tale the old, blind Tobit sends his son Tobias to Gabael to recover some money he had left with him. The road is dangerous and Tobias, who doesn't know the way, hires a guide named Azariah (which means "helped by God"). Tobias doesn't know that the unknown guide is in fact the angel Raphael, sent by God to accompany him. As they journey, Azariah takes a detour. Rather than taking Tobias to Gabael, he leads him to Raguel, the father of Sarah with whom

---

8. Ian Hislop, cited by Timothy Radcliffe in *What is the Point of Being a Christian?* (London: Burns & Oates, 2005), p. 25.

9. Edgar Allan Poe, "A Dream Within a Dream" in *Complete Tales & Poems* (New Jersey: Castle Books, 2002), pp. 793–794.

Tobias falls in love and marries. In the end, they don't go to Gabael together at all. During the wedding festivities, Tobias sends Azariah to get the money. He then returns home, filled with joy, along with the angel, Sarah, and his dog, to cure his father Tobit's blindness. This Biblical tale shows us how God accomplished his plan of love, by way of Tobit's own intentions and his son's obedience. He desired to save Tobit and Sara, and he used Tobit's plans as an opportunity to carry out his greater intention.

At its heart, the whole Bible speaks to us of how God accomplishes his divine plan through man's ambitions. God had a plan for humanity at the beginning of the world: "Let us make man in our image, after our likeness" (Gen 1:26). He created human beings who are themselves capable of creative works. As they engage in these works, they cooperate with God's plans. King David, for example, dreamed of building a temple for God, but it was his son, Solomon, who constructed it. When we think about it, Solomon's temple was itself only the dream within a greater dream—it foreshadowed the true Temple of God. David didn't know it, but the temple he dreamed of was God's dream, the Body of Christ, the Church. A dream within the dream of a dream!

3. The Quiet Strength of Desire

Our awareness of being at the service of a dream greater than our own should not lead us away from planning and dreaming. On the contrary, it should lead us to do it with more intensity, and more peacefully, with an ardent calm. We should be enthusiastic, but with a certain detachment from the seriousness of our endeavors. God can work in our lives just as well through successes as through apparent failures. We must have a certain indifference about the result.

German philosopher Eugen Herrigel demonstrates this in his book *Zen in the Art of Archery*, as he recounts the different phases of his initiation into Japanese archery (Kyūdō) in Sendai. He explains how this practice requires that the archer hit the mark without having aimed at it, losing sight of both the goal and the desire to attain it.[10] His teacher says to him, for example: "Don't think of what you have to do, don't consider how to carry it out! . . . The shot will only go smoothly when it takes the archer himself by surprise. It must be as if the bowstring suddenly cut through the thumb that held it. You musn't open the right hand

---

10. Eugen Herrigel, *Zen in the Art of Archery* (New York: Random House, 1971), pp. 63–64.

on purpose."[11] Or again: "The right art is purposeless, aimless! . . . What stands in your way is that you have a much too willful will."[12]

This might seem contradictory, considering what we said earlier about how important it is to have a clear vision of the why and the how of our actions. However, this is not really the case. What Herrigel speaks about does not affect the aim of the shot, nor the mastery of the action. It simply seeks to achieve it with the least tension possible, as naturally as possible, with grace and with confidence.

---

11. Eugen Herrigel, *Zen in the Art of Archery*, p. 31.
12. Eugen Herrigel, *Zen in the Art of Archery*, p. 34.

6

Confidence

"I can do all things in him who strengthens me."[1]

—St. Paul

IF WE WANT TO ACHIEVE our great desires, we must dare to seize the reins and jump into action. We must envision potential victory. We must have confidence. And yet, we all struggle with confidence. We doubt too much. We get easily used to the form of nihilism that we might call quiet despair, or chronic defeatism.

Psychologist Martin Seligman talks about "learned helplessness."[2] He carried out a rather cruel experiment on three groups of dogs. One group was subjected to light electric shocks that they could stop by pressing a pedal, one group was subjected to the shocks but they could not stop them, and a third control

1. Phil 4:13.

2. See Martin Seligman, *Helplessness: On Depression, Development, and Death* (San Francisco: Freeman, 1975).

group were not subjected to any shocks. Next, Seligman and his team placed the dogs in a box from which they could escape by jumping over a slightly elevated barrier. At the moment of the electric shock, the first and third groups jumped over the barrier, while the second group remained in the box, subject to the electric shocks. They had learned to be helpless! Seligman repeated this same kind of experiment, including with humans (who were subjected to loud noises with an on/off switch), and concluded that when we have experienced defeat several times, we become quickly resigned to it and no longer try to remove ourselves from difficult situations.[3] All athletes at a high level know that belief in success is an essential condition for that success. The same is true on a spiritual level: faith and confidence in Jesus is the solid ground on which our Christian ambition stands.

But what is this confidence? What is its object? Should we have confidence in ourselves or in God? And to what extent should we have confidence in others? Finally—and this is essential—how can we grow in confidence?

---

3. For a detailed description of this experiment, see J. Bruce Overmier and Martin Seligman, "Effects of inescapable shock upon subsequent escape and avoidance learning," *Journal of Comparative and Physiological Psychology*, 1967, no. 63, pp. 28–33.

1. What is Confidence?

Confidence is nothing other than a powerful hope based on the firm opinion that it is possible to attain our goal.[4] This definition, taken from St. Thomas Aquinas, begins with the general notion of a robust hope (*spes roborata*), and adds that its robustness is founded in the belief that "yes, it's possible." Etymology confirms this definition; the word "confidence" (*fiducia* in Latin) comes from the verb "to have trust in" (*confidere*), in which we find *cum* ("with") and *fidere* ("to trust").[5] For example, if we undertake an expedition to climb Mount Everest, we must have confidence in experienced guides and sherpas. We will have to entrust ourselves to them. This is only possible if we think they are trustworthy enough, worthy of our confidence, competent, and good-hearted.

2. Who Should We Trust?

We can have confidence in many areas: primarily in ourselves, in God, in others, or in all three together.

4. See Aquinas, *Summa Theologica*, 2-3.129.6: *Fiducia est spes roborata ex aliqua firma opinione* (see also article 6, ad 2, and ad 3).

5. See *Merriam Webster's Collegiate Dictionary*, 11th Edition, s.v. "confidence."

Let's return to the example of climbing Mount Everest. We first believe we are capable of it (confidence in ourselves) along with the competence of our guides (confidence in others), and with God's help (confidence in God).

There is, of course, a form of self-confidence that is absurd, known as presumption. Not just anybody can do every possible thing. A presumptuous man believes he is capable of doing great things when he is not. As St. Thomas says, ". . . all foolish and thoughtless persons attempt everything and are full of hope."[6] Aristotle remarked that people who are drunk "become sanguine."[7]

The presumptuous man exaggerates his prediction of victory, often to the point of lacking vigilance or caution. He is so sure of his own capabilities that he forgets the unknowns of reality and the risks of existence. The story of the last judicial duel in France is a dramatic illustration of this. On July 10th, 1547, Guy Chabot de Jarnac confronted François de Vivonne for some ridiculous reason. As François de Vivonne knew himself to be the very best fencer, he had already

6. Aquinas, *Summa Theologica*, 1-2.40.6.

7. Artistotle, *Ethics*, trans. J.A.K. Thompson (London: Penguin Books, 1976), 3.8.1117a14.

prepared a superb feast to celebrate his victory. However, Jarnac caught him with an unprecedented hit to the back of his knee, which Vivonne was not expecting. The presumptuous man anticipates victory as though it has already happened, forgetting that it hasn't happened yet. Even though we may be very gifted and competent, we must not forget two things: humility and vigilance.

We must be aware and truthful about our capabilities and what is realistic and what isn't, or else we risk either being timid or presumptuous. The presumptuous man thinks he is capable when he is not. The timid man judges himself incapable even when he is. Aristotle notes that the timid man is worse than a fool, suggesting that his lack of ambition comes more from a lack of energy or desire than from being unaware of his potential.[8]

Having said this, a question remains for the Christian. Is confidence in oneself not always presumption? Jesus said, "Apart from me you can do nothing" (Jn 15:5). If we take Christ's statement seriously, shouldn't we consider it a bad thing to have confidence in ourselves? Shouldn't we have confidence in God alone? It seems to me that drawing such a

8. Aristotle, *Ethics*, 4.3.1125a23–24.

conclusion threatens our human and psychological balance. Self-confidence is necessary for our well-being. It would be better to say that having confidence in ourselves is to trust in the gifts that God has given us, and therefore, indirectly, to trust in God. As Marcel Viller said, "Self-confidence is legitimate, as long as it can be reduced to confidence in God. If we trust in the gifts God has given us, we trust indirectly in God. Self-confidence is reproachable and idiotic if it is excluded from confidence in God."[9]

3. How to Boost our Confidence

Nobody aspires to things that seem impossible. To boost our ambition, we must find ways to enlarge our perception of what is possible. Two factors will help us grow in confidence: growing our real potential for success, and growing our awareness of this potential. We may lack confidence either because we are in fact unable to succeed (which can be corrected by working to make ourselves capable), or because we judge ourselves to be incapable even when we are. Growth in self-confidence relies on two things: growth in potential, and growth in awareness of our potential.

---

9. Marcel Viller, "Confiance," in *Dictionnaire de Spiritualité Ascétique et Mystique*, vol. 2, (Paris: Beauchesnes, 1953), 1411–1412. Our translation.

The timid man sees himself as incapable even when he is; the presumptuous man thinks he is capable when he is not. The realist judges himself to be capable of what he can, in fact, accomplish, either by himself or with someone else's help. His awareness of his own potential allows him to affirm his personal greatness in the sight of others, and to take his rightful place without needing to usurp anyone else.

So, we must first work hard to grow our potential for success. Through hard work and experience, we can come to believe that it's possible to do the very thing that once seemed impossible. This is how we grow in confidence, no longer afraid of doing those things we are certain we can do.

7

A Fighting Spirit

"Say to us, as once Horace would have said,
Whether man must fight or follow his destiny?"[1]
—Alphonse de Lamartine

WE WOULD LIKE FOR LIFE to be like a long, tranquil river. Unfortunately, this isn't so. From our birth to our dying breath, there is a struggle to be fought. We must mobilize our audacity, our courage, and even our anger, to fight it well. The philosopher Alain says that ambition is "a passion resulting from anger, which is produced when our efforts meet resistance."[2] The passion to succeed, motivated by irascibility, pushes us to overcome the obstacles in our way.[3]

---

1. Alphonse de Lamartine, *Méditations poétiques, Œuvre de Lamartine* (Paris, 1860), 1, p. 217. Our translation.

2. Alain, *Définitions* (Paris: Gallimard, 1953), p. 22. Our translation.

3. The word "irascible" comes from the Latin verb *irascor* (to be angry), and refers to the capacity to become angry, to find within oneself the energy to fight.

The Bible constantly sings the praises of those who fight in a good way, and for a good cause. We are told, for example, of David's soldiers "whose faces were like the faces of lions, and who were swift as gazelles upon the mountains" (1 Chr 12:8). A good and strong irascibility strengthens our courage and helps us achieve our ambitions, despite the struggles we will face.

"Anger . . . [is] sweeter far than flowing honey," said Homer.[4] This is not so, of course, but there is a certain joy in acting from our irascibility. It's not a sort of masochism, nor stoicism. It's not a sacrificial spirituality, or a spirituality of mortification or belligerence. Rather, it is the intrinsic joy of the struggle for a result we know we will attain. This is one of the hidden aspects of St. Paul's words: "Rejoice in your hope" (Rom 12:12).

An athlete trains to his limit, but in competition to win, goes beyond those limits. The same is true in the spiritual domain. If we never go beyond our limits in faith, if we never take risks for God, we will stagnate. God wants to work miracles in our lives, he wants to respond to our great ambitions and make us witnesses to his marvels. To do this, he desires our cooperation

---

4. See Homer, *The Iliad*, trans. Alston Hurd Chase and William G. Perry Jr. (Boston: Little, Brown & Co., 1950), bk. 18, p. 331.

by taking risks for him—particularly risks that take effort. When Peter and his companions were exhausted after a night at sea, casting their nets again and again without catching anything, Jesus said to them: "Put out into the deep and let down your nets for a catch" (Lk 5:1–10). The catch was miraculous!

1. Conquering the Lion

St. Peter describes the devil as a roaring lion that prowls around us, coming and going, ready to devour us (1 Pt 5:8). How better to describe that we are always engaged in a fight? The tiger and the lion are the biggest felines we know, but the lion is the only one crowned with a mane, which explains why the lion is often used as a symbol of royal power. However, its muscular strength and penchant for nighttime activities have made it a particular symbol for the devil, the "prince of this world." To go up against a lion and win makes for a real feat![5]

The Biblical figure, Benai'ah, was one of David's warriors, who, "went down and slew a lion in a pit on a day when snow had fallen" (2 Sm 23:20). If you saw a lion coming toward you, your normal reflex would be

---

5. See Jgs 14:5–18; 1 Sm 17:34–37 and Sir 47:3; 2 Sm 23:20 and 1 Chr 11:22.

to run away. But lion hunters do the opposite. Rather than staring at a danger advancing upon them, they see an opportunity for glory. They don't flee; they engage in the fight.[6] This might not be the most prudent idea ever, but nevertheless, in the Bible the killing of a lion is mentioned several times as a demonstration of particularly distinguished courage. We might think of Samson. The Book of Judges tells us that one day, "a young lion roared against him; and the Spirit of the Lord came mightily upon him, and he tore the lion asunder as one tears a kid; and he had nothing in his hand" (Jgs 14:5–6). Or David's declaration to Saul as he went to battle against the giant Goliath:

> Your servant used to keep sheep for his father; and when there came a lion, or a bear, and took a lamb from the flock, I went after him and smote him and delivered it out of his mouth; and if he arose against me, I caught him by his beard, and smote him and killed him. Your servant has killed both lions and bears; and this uncircumcised Philistine shall be like one of them, seeing he has defied the armies of the living God. (1 Sm 17:34–36)

---

6. Here, I am inspired by Mark Batterson's book, *Chase the Lion*. The subtitle is significant: *If Your Dream Doesn't Scare You, It's Too Small.*

However, in Benai'ah's case, a particular detail stands out. We are told he went down into a pit to fight a lion "on a day when snow had fallen." Why this detail about the unfavorable weather? Napoleon allegedly said that there are two types of courage: normal courage, and courage at two in the morning. Going down into a pit to fight a lion on a snowy day is clearly an example of the second type of courage. Think for a minute about how this fight, whether real or fictional, might have been. We're not talking about a circus. A lion weighs between 440 and 550 pounds. It can run up to fifty miles per hour. It can jump ten feet in height and thirty-six feet in distance. If one day you find yourself in a pit with a lion in front of you, the least that can be said is that you have a problem. If the weather is cold on top of it, that is what we call a bad day. However, if the Bible commends Benai'ah for going down into a pit to take out a lion, then it wasn't a day for running away. There are times when running away isn't the right option. We must go for it! We must fight the lion. And we must put God in between us and it.

If Benai'ah had looked for an excuse to refuse the fight, he could easily have found one and nobody would have reproached him for it. However, his ambition sought out an opportunity for action, rather than an excuse to flee. We must do the same if we wish to achieve our ambition of sainthood, focusing on opportunities to glorify God rather than excuses to get out of difficulty. We must put God between ourselves and our problems.

Sooner or later, we will find ourselves face to face with our fears, and this is when it all plays out. In the end, do we not pity those who spend their time running from their problems, who have become masters in the art of evasion? Life is a fight. Benai'ah's fight against the lion, moreover, decided his whole life. The Scripture passage tells us, "These things did Benai'ah . . . And David set him over his bodyguard" (2 Sm 23:22–23). He became the head of David's bodyguard. Not bad! A saying goes: "No guts, no glory!" Benai'ah had both.

2. Overcoming Discouragement

A little voice in us can't help but believe the saying of Simon de Bignicourt: "Life is a struggle that man has lost in advance."[7] It's true that no matter what we do, we will die one day, and grow old before that. But if this is the case, what good is it to struggle so much? Why should we spend our life fighting, if final defeat is certain? Solomon himself, after so many amazing

7. Simon de Bignicourt (a moralist, and friend of Diderot), *Pensées diverses et réflexions philosophiques, propres à former l'esprit et le cœur* (London: 1755). Our translation.

works and successes, seems discouraged in the famous verse attributed to him, "Vanity of vanities! All is vanity. What does man gain by all the toil at which he toils under the sun?" (Eccl 1:2–3).

Christian faith invites us to believe that victory is certain, no matter how things seem. "I will not be discouraged!" said Thérèse of the Child Jesus.[8] Why? Because Christ is risen. Despite the semblance of defeat, victory is certain in that God's name will be glorified, his kingdom will come, and his will be done, the bread of our life will be given to us, we will be forgiven, freed from temptations, and delivered from evil! If we accept the fight, God's ambition will be realized in us. Here are three examples from the Bible:

Let us consider Joseph, the patriarch of Genesis. His is the story of a man who had great dreams. I remember a businessman in Dallas who told me that, for him, this Biblical hero incarnated the "American Dream." Joseph went from being a country dweller from an unknown family in Canaan to Egypt's secretary of state. Egypt was the most powerful and civilized nation in the Middle East at that time. Yet his life was so full of failures!

---

8. Thérèse's resolution on the day of her First Communion, May 8, 1884. *Vie thérésienne* (Liseux: Pèlerinage de Lisieux), no. 74, p. 134. Our translation.

Reading his story, we can't help but pity poor Joseph, but we also see how God's hand was upon him. Every apparent failure guided him to exactly the place he needed to go, according to God's plan, and this is what allowed him to save his family from famine. This "man of dreams" had to learn realism. He saw his ideals shatter and he left the realm of his imagination, but he did not stop believing in God's dream for him. He discovered that the strength of youth was not enough for God's plans to be fulfilled, but that he had to go from failure to failure to reach victory.

How did Joseph persevere? He remained focused on God. He continued to attribute all to God. At the end of Genesis, he consoles his own brothers who had sold him as a slave for a few coins:

> "Fear not, for am I in the place of God? As for you, you meant evil against me; but God meant it for good, to bring it about that many people should be kept alive, as they are today. So do not fear; I will provide for you and your little ones." Thus he reassured them and comforted them. (Gn 50:19–21)

The prophet Jeremiah's life is another example of the struggle against discouragement. He lived during a horrendous time when the people had lost sight of God, and there he was, sent by God to announce coming catastrophes in the kingdom: King Nebuchadnezzar's conquest of Jerusalem and the exile to Babylon. His prophecy was not received well, and he ended up in prison. During his whole ministry, he never experienced the success of his preaching. He was called to a ministry of apparent failure! Jeremiah was discouraged at times, but an interior strength compelled him to continue. He was incapable of stopping his mission, almost despite himself. He was like a lion when he prophesied, afraid of nothing and nobody, his heart burning with divine ardor, filled with enthusiasm! Despite his failings, he exclaims:

> Ah Lord God! It is thou who hast made the heavens and the earth by thy great power and by thy outstretched arm! Nothing is too hard for thee . . . O great and mighty God whose name is the Lord of hosts. . . . (Jer 32:17–18)

Joshua, whose name in Hebrew corresponds to that of Jesus, spent his entire life fighting. It was Joshua who led the people of Israel across the Jordan to enter the Promised Land, after which he spent most of his time fighting enemies. He is one of the greatest heroes of the Bible, and when he reached old age, he was seized with a desire to ease off the pace. But the Lord says to him:

> You are old and advanced in years, and there remains yet very much land to be possessed. This is the land that yet remains: all the regions of the Philistines, and all those of the Gesh′urites (from the Shihor, which is east of Egypt, northward to the boundary of Ekron [)] . . . all the land of the Canaanites . . . to Aphek, to the boundary of the Amorites, and the land of the Geb′alites, and all Lebanon, toward the sunrising, from Ba′al-gad below Mount Hermon to the entrance of Hamath. (Jos 13:1–5)

Joshua was familiar with the temptation to give up the fight. The spirit for conquest tends to decrease with age, either because of greater fatigue or diminished capacity to recuperate. Joshua could have made his excuses, saying, "I'm too old now, I've fought enough." Some of us, too, after years of Christian life, might experience the temptation to give up. "I'm well aware that there are areas of my life that haven't yet been totally given over to Christ, but I'm tired of doing battle. I've already fought so much." Joshua sets a remarkable example for us. Despite his age, he takes a stand before the people:

> And if you be unwilling to serve the Lord, choose this day whom you will serve, whether the gods your

> fathers served in the region beyond the River, or the gods of the Amorites in whose land you dwell; but as for me and my house, we will serve the Lord. (Jos 24:15)

Here we see Joshua's greatness of soul, and therefore his youthfulness, for the two go together. We remain young as long as we see and desire greatness. God desires for us to be young; he wants to make us sons and daughters full of hope. This is why he taught us to turn toward him and call him *Our Father*.

PART THREE

God's Seven Ambitions for Us

"Lead thou me to the rock that is higher than I."
—Ps 61:2

IN PART ONE, we saw that God created us like children who desire to be great. In Part Two, we considered the three attitudes we must develop so that our hopes for greatness might become more practical. But God calls us to heights that are too high for us, and we need his help. This is why Christian ambition is fundamentally trained through prayer. We will discuss this now.

Jesus gave us the perfect prayer, the *Our Father*.[1] It is the most powerful and wise prayer of all, because it is his own. It summarizes everything that God wishes us to ask of him, and therefore all his ambitions for us.

1. We find this prayer announced twice in the New Testament: in Mt 6:9–13, and in Lk 11:1–4. In Luke's version there are only five petitions, while Matthew has seven. Many scholars have sought to understand why. Here, we will content ourselves to comment on Matthew's version, which the Church has chosen for its liturgy.

Tertullian said that it is "an epitome of the whole Gospel."[2] Indeed it is so, with a sense of hope. It teaches us to ask for the seven gifts God wants to give us. When we pray the *Our Father*, we take God's ambition for us as our own.

To better understand this, we will first highlight the wisdom of how the various petitions of the *Our Father* are ordered. Then we will examine the meaning of each petition. Finally, we will look at the central and fundamental intention of the *Our Father:* that the reality on earth might reflect that of heaven.

2. Tertullian. "Concerning Prayer," in *Tertullian's Treatises*, trans. Alexander Souter (London: The Macmillan Company, 1919), p. 21.

8

The Ordering of the *Our Father*

"In the Lord's Prayer not only do we ask
for all that we may rightly desire,
but also in the order
wherein we ought to desire them."[1]
—St. Thomas Aquinas

WE USUALLY DIVIDE the *Our Father* into two parts: the first three petitions (conjugated in the second-person singular, "you"), and the four final petitions (in the first-person plural, "we"). This classic division contains a rich first teaching: when we pray, we must first think of God, and then of ourselves. His name, his reign, and his will come first; and only then comes the rest: our bread, the forgiveness of our trespasses, our victory over temptation, and our deliverance from evil. This wise ordering corresponds with the Lord's counsel to: "Seek first his kingdom and his righteousness,

1. Aquinas, *Summa Theologica*, 2-2.83.9.

and all these things shall be yours as well" (Mt 6:33). Pope Benedict XVI compared the two parts of the *Our Father* to the two tablets of the Ten Commandments, which themselves correspond to the two commandments of love (for God and for our neighbor). "The *Our Father,*" he says, "begins with God and then, from that starting point, shows us the way toward being human. At the end we descend to the ultimate threat besetting man, for whom the Evil One lies in wait."[2]

I would like to suggest another way of presenting the *Our Father*, which shows how the ordering of the seven petitions summarizes the essentials we must hope for in order to live well.[3] For this, we will distinguish three parts:

1. In the first two petitions, Jesus teaches us to desire all that truly gives meaning to our whole lives: the sanctification of the Father's name, and the pursuit of his kingdom. God's ambition for us is clearly that we first wholeheartedly desire his glory, and that we rejoice in it both now and in eternity. He desires that we love him with our whole hearts, and that

2. Pope Benedict XVI, *Jesus of Nazareth*, vol. 1 (New York: Doubleday, 2007), p. 134.

3. Here, I will return to Thomas Aquinas' presentation of the *Our Father* in his *Summa Theologica* (see 2-2.83.9).

we love ourselves in him. So, we have the first petition, "Hallowed be thy name," which expresses our desire for God's glory, and then the second petition, "Thy kingdom come," which expresses our desire to attain to this same glory ourselves. The other five petitions concern *how* to achieve this goal.

2. The third and fourth petitions pertain to the means necessary for attaining this goal: the accomplishment of God's will and the possession of the material goods that we need (symbolized by bread). When we do his will, we cooperate with the coming of his kingdom and bring about the sanctification of his name. It goes without saying that this is the only adequate way to glorify God. However, to see our mission through we must also receive our "daily bread," whether we understand this to be the Eucharist which sustains us on our way to heaven, or material bread, a symbol of all that fulfills our needs. So, we have the third petition: "Your will be done on earth as it is in heaven," followed by, "Give us this day our daily bread."
3. Petitions five, six, and seven concern the different aspects of spiritual combat: forgiveness, avoidance of temptations, and deliverance from evil in general and the devil in particular. These petitions concern everything that must be removed from our path so that we can reach our objective. The first is sin which, by

definition, causes us to miss the goal of our life. This is why we ask the Lord to forgive our trespasses. Next is temptation, which causes us to stray from the right path, and therefore the sixth petition: "Lead us not into temptation." Finally, the devil himself is the first to tempt us and lead us astray through sin, so we have the final petition: "Deliver us from evil."

This ordering of the petitions seems logical. It teaches us to ask first for the objective, and then for the means to get there. As for the means, we ask first for the direct means (God's will and bread, both necessary to attain our goal), and then for the indirect ones (the removal of those obstacles that could cause us to miss the mark of our life).

Now let us turn to an analysis of these seven petitions. Here I will draw on St. Augustine's profound intuition, developed several centuries later by St. Thomas Aquinas. In his commentary on the Sermon on the Mount, St. Augustine highlights the connection between each petition of the *Our Father* and one of the seven gifts of the Holy Spirit,[4] as well as one of

4. As a reminder: "The seven gifts of the Holy Spirit are wisdom, understanding, counsel, fortitude, knowledge, piety, and fear of the Lord." *Catechism of the Catholic Church*, 2nd ed. (Washington, DC: Libreria Editrice Vaticana–United States Conference of Catholic Bishops, 2000), 1831.

the seven Beatitudes.[5] He says, "The sevenfold number of these petitions [of the *Our Father*] also seems to me to correspond to that sevenfold number out of which the whole sermon [on the Mount] before us has had its rise."[6]

The main point of this approach, which might seem overly systematic, is to help us understand the extent of God's ambition that we live fully in the Holy Spirit in order to find beatitude in him. Happy are they who live out the Holy Spirit's seven ambitions for them! In fact, St. Augustine's use of the number seven is not all that artificial; the Jerusalem Bible notes regarding the seven petitions of the *Our Father*: "The Lord's Prayer in its Matthaean form has seven petitions. The number is a favorite of Matthew's: two times seven

---

5. See Augustine, *Augustine on the Sermon on the Mount*, found in *Nicene and Post-Nicene Fathers, First Series,* vol. 6, trans. William Findlay, ed. Philip Schaff (Buffalo, NY: Christian Literature Publishing, 1888). There are eight beatitudes, but Augustine considers the final one ("Blessed are those who are persecuted . . .") as a summary of the first seven. In his commentary on Psalm 12, he writes "For seven steps also of beatitude there are, which the Lord goes over, according to Matthew, in the same sermon which he spoke on the Mount. . . . Of which seven sentences, it may be observed how all that long sermon was spoken. For the eighth where it is said, 'Blessed are they who suffer persecution for righteousness' sake' denotes the fire itself, whereby the silver is proved seven times." For Augustine, the number seven signifies wholeness and perfection (see, for example, *The City of God*, 1.20.5.3).

6. Augustine, *Sermon on the Mount*, 2.11.38.

generations in the Genealogy (1:17), seven Beatitudes, (5:4e), seven parables (13:3b), forgiveness not seven but seventy-seven times (18:22), seven diatribes against the Pharisees (23:13h), seven sections into which the Gospel is divided."[7] It is a distinctive number: in its addition of three (the number of the Trinity) and four (the number of creation: north, south, east, and west), it symbolizes the fruit of the union of Creator and creature. It follows the example of the number twelve (three times four), which expresses the fruitful multiplication of the union between God and the world, and which is also the symbolic number of the Church *par excellence* (for example, the twelve apostles).

7. Jerusalem Bible (New York: Doubleday, 1990), Mt 6:9, note b.

9

The Seven Petitions

"The promises of the Lord are promises that are pure, silver refined in a furnace on the ground, purified seven times."

—Ps 12:6

1. "Hallowed Be Thy Name"

(Living the Gift of Fear of the Lord)

Meaning of the First Petition

To understand how this first petition expresses God's fundamental ambition for us, we must first understand the significance of the verb "to hallow" and the concept of "name," both less familiar to us now than in Jesus' time.

The Greek term we usually translate as "hallowed" in the *Our Father* is *hagiostheto*. In this verb, we find the word *hagios* which means "holy" or "sacred," in the sense of being set apart, of being glorified. The action of sanctifying God, of hallowing him, of glorifying him refers to a movement of adoration made by the creature who recognizes the grandeur of his creator, his transcendence, his glory, and his infinite majesty.

During the Mass, we enter liturgically into this sanctification of the name of God when we proclaim "Holy, Holy, Holy (three times *hagios*) lord God of power and might. Heaven and earth are filled with your glory." We could therefore translate the first petition of the *Our Father* like this: "May thy name be recognized as sacred," or: "Consecrated be thy name," or, as suggested by Father Jean Carmignac, "Glorified be thy name."[1]

God obviously does not need us to sanctify him. He is perfectly holy within himself. The first petition, therefore, does not mean to somehow give God a surplus of holiness, which would be absurd, but that we ourselves might be sanctified. We are, in fact, asking God to sanctify his name in us. It is as though we were to ask, "Father, may your name be holy in us and through us." This is God's original ambition for us: "Let us make man in our image, after our likeness" (Gn 1:26). God is holy by nature, and he wants us to be holy through grace. This was his call to his people in

---

1. Jean Carmignac, *À l'écoute du Notre Père* (Paris: Éditions de Paris, 1969), p. 27. Our translation.

Leviticus: "You shall be holy; for I the Lord your God am holy" (Lev 19:2).

Theologians tell us that we do not cause God's intrinsic (*ad intra*) glory to grow, but that it will be more greatly manifested *ad extra* (to others) if our lives are holy. Therefore, we ask God for the grace to live in such a way that our works might make his name to be seen as holy. God will not be made more holy himself, of course, but if his holiness takes hold of us, it will become great in us, and it will be sanctified, or "hallowed," through us. But why refer to his name? Jesus could have taught us to say: "Our Father in heaven, may you be hallowed." This would have been simpler. Why add this notion of name that was no doubt meaningful for the Jews of that time, but clearly less so for us? Perhaps it is because his name suggests the idea of renown, and therefore sanctification *ad extra*. A person's name refers to them, but in relation to others. God in himself cannot be sanctified; he is already infinitely holy. His name, however, can be, if we make it renowned through our lives. This is what the first petition of the *Our Father* means: "May your name be sanctified, Lord! May it be sanctified through my life!" May those who are not holy become saints, and may those who are holy persevere in holiness, and may those who are on the journey be purified day by day to become "holy and blameless" in the presence of the Lord.[2] This is God's fundamental ambition for us, and the goal of our lives: ". . . just as the name of God is holy, so we may obtain his holiness in our souls."[3]

Fear of the Lord and Poverty of Spirit

St. Augustine says that when we pray in this way, we call upon that gift of the Holy Spirit which we call "fear of the Lord." As St. Thomas Aquinas explains in his commentary on the *Our Father*: ". . . He works in us the gift of holy fear; and by that gift we pray when we say, hallowed be thy name."[4]

It is fitting for this petition to be the first, since "The fear of the Lord is the beginning of wisdom."[5] Every gift from heaven requires us to be first turned toward God and away from evil. As we read in Proverbs, "by the fear of the Lord a man avoids evil" (Prv

---

2. Eph 1:4: "Even as he chose us in him before the foundation of the world, that we should be holy and blameless before him."

3. St Peter Chrysologus, *Sermo* 71; cited in the *Catechism of the Catholic Church*, 2814.

4. Aquinas, *The Lord's Prayer*, trans. Fr. Rawes, D.D. (London: Burns and Oates, 1879), no. 8, p. 38.

5. This affirmation is repeated frequently in the Bible, for example: Prv 9:10; Ps 111:10; Jb 28:28, among others.

16:6). When we experience this gift and are seized by divine majesty, we submit ourselves spontaneously to him and by instinct we push away anything that might offend him. We find our life synchronized according to God. He sets it right again.

From the perspective of our reflections on ambition, we could say that divine fear is the fear of limiting God's ambition for us, of being an obstacle to him, or of not being responsive. So, here is the first thing to ask of the Lord, as he taught us himself: the fulfillment of his ambition for us, the coming of his holiness, his kingdom, within us. For this to happen, we must be very poor in spirit, and accept to be made even poorer by the holiness of his presence that overtakes us. "Blessed are the poor in spirit, for theirs is the kingdom of heaven" (Mt 5:3).

2. "Thy Kingdom Come"

(Living the Gift of Piety)

Meaning of the Second Petition

In this petition, we recognize that God is our "king" and we express our desire for him to reign over the world, over our whole lives, our activities, and our environment. In fact, the Greek word used here (*basileia*, corresponding to the Hebrew *malkout*), refers to royal power. When we ask for the kingdom of God, we ask that everyone might acknowledge his lordship. This is a reasonable request, because we know that wherever God does not reign, things return to chaos. When the Lord no longer governs our hearts, they turn quickly to the Prince of Darkness.

However, this petition might seem ambiguous, because our ideas of royalty are very human. Every religious fanatic dreams that God will come definitively as king, so that the world might be at peace—and the result is always a disaster! Jesus clearly didn't invite us to pray that the Father's reign would come in the form of a dictatorship! When Pilate asked him if he claimed to be the king of the Jews, Jesus clearly responded, "My kingship is not of this world; if my kingship were of this world, my servants would fight, that I might not be handed over to the Jews; but my kingship is not from the world" (Jn 18:36).

So, what is this hoped-for "reign"? What does it really mean? I believe that it will ultimately be the coming of the Good Shepherd himself. This idea impressed itself upon me as I compared different translations of Psalm 23. I was surprised to see that the Vulgate translates the first verse, "The Lord is my shepherd" as *Dominus Reget me* ("The Lord governs me"). The Latin verb *Regere* led to the word *Rex* (king). This translation is far removed from the original Hebrew text, transforming the shepherd into a king! Seen inversely, however, this "error of translation" tells us a lot about royalty in the Gospel. The shepherd is not so much a king, as the king is, in fact, a shepherd! St. Jerome's translation helps us to understand that God's reign really means caring for his sheep. The king is a shepherd, and his royal domain is like a sheepfold.

What we are asking for in the second petition is a reign of tenderness and mercy. This is precisely God's ambition for us: to see us accept his love and live fully from it. This is the divine ambition we desire when we pray, "Thy kingdom come."

But we must go even further. If truth be told, the work of a human shepherd is always a little ambiguous. He loves his sheep, he cares for them, but in the end, he will sell them—or eat them! That's not how the Lord loves us. He loves us and takes care of us, without any exceptions. To prove it to us, so that we might have no fear of him, he even made himself one of us: not only a good shepherd, but a lamb. And as a lamb he intends to guide us. The book of Revelation tells us it will always be this way: "For the Lamb in the midst of the throne will be their shepherd, and he will guide them to springs of living water" (Rv 7:17).

The Gift of Piety and Meekness

St. Thomas Aquinas, drawing on St. Augustine, links this petition to the gift of piety:

> Now piety properly is a sweet and loving affection for our father, and for everyone who is suffering. Since therefore God is our father, as is plain, we must not only reverence him and fear him, but also have for him an affection of sweetness and loving regard. It is this loving affection which leads us to pray that the kingdom of God may come. . . .[6]

Piety is a filial affection for God. Through the gift of piety, the Holy Spirit permits us to live in familiarity with God, without removing any of the respect due to him. Too much familiarity in human relationships can be detrimental to respect, but the same is not true in relationship with God. "For the more intimate we become with God through love and contemplation, realizing how superior he is, the more we respect him and the less do we esteem ourselves."[7]

---

6. Aquinas, *The Lord's Prayer*, no. 8, p. 38.

7. Aquinas, *Commentary on the Gospel of St. John*, part 1: chapters 1–7, trans. James A. Weisheipl, O.P. (New York: Magi Books, 1980), no. 666.

A certain gentleness flows from this filial sense of piety, and so it corresponds well to the beatitude: "Blessed are the meek, for they shall inherit the earth" (Mt 5:5). Gentleness brings to mind docility. The docility of the Lord's sheep allows them to be led without opposition or anger. The words "for they shall inherit the earth" remind us of Abraham, who left everything, and in docility followed the Lord to the Promised Land. We must be meek to pray in truth: "Thy kingdom come." Reciprocally, when we let God reign in our lives, we become docile.

The first two petitions of the *Our Father* express God's fundamental ambition for us: the Lord wants our lives to glorify him, and that his glory might also be within us. These two petitions convey the blend of majesty and tenderness that is particular to Christianity. We must both adore God and welcome him as a lamb. This was the experience for Mary and Joseph at Christmas. In a surprising play written in 1940, the existentialist playwright Jean-Paul Sartre transmits his sense of this to us, though he himself was a nonbeliever. He was detained for some months in a French prison camp in Germany, alongside several priests who asked him to write a meditation for Christmas Eve. Sartre accepted, and perceived this mélange of fear and piety that permeates the Christian mystery:

> The Virgin is pale, and she looks at the child. . . . She carried him for nine months. She nursed him and her milk became the blood of God. She clasps him in her arms and says to him, "my little one!" But at other moments she remains speechless, and she thinks: "God is here," and she feels herself seized with a religious fear before this God who cannot yet speak, before this infant . . . for he is God, and he surpasses every limit that she can imagine. It is a harsh trial for a mother, to feel fear for herself and her human condition before her son. But I think there are other moments, quick and fleeting, when she senses both that Christ is her son, her little one, and that he is God. She looks at him and she thinks: "This God is my child! This divine flesh is my flesh, he is made of me, he has my eyes, and the shape of his mouth is my own. He resembles me; he is God and he resembles me." And no woman has had it so—her God for her alone. A little God, who can be carried in her arms and covered with kisses, a God who is warm and who smiles and breathes, a God who can be touched and who lives. . . .[8]

8. This passage is taken from Jean-Paul Sartre's first theatrical play, titled *Barounia ou le Fils du tonnerre,* fifth tableau, scene three. See M. Contat et M. Rybalka: *Les écrits de Sartre* (Paris: Gallimard, 1970), pp. 616–617. Our translation.

Christian ambition is first turned toward the Father: "Seek first his kingdom and his righteousness" (Mt 6:33). We see this demonstrated in the first two petitions of the *Our Father*. Now, let us consider the means necessary to fulfill our desire. We will begin with those which provide us with all that we need to reach our goal: obedience to God, who is mainly responsible for getting us there and who leads us directly ("Thy will be done, on earth as it is in heaven"), and the tools that can help us along the way ("Give us this day our daily bread").

3. "Thy Will be Done"

(LIVING THE GIFT OF KNOWLEDGE)

Meaning of the Third Petition

The third petition is translated like this: "Thy will be done on earth, as it is in heaven." However, the verb "to do" is not found in the Greek text. A more literal translation would be: "May thy will as in heaven be also on earth." We can, of course, keep the translation we are used to, and which sounds better in the liturgy. But we must understand that it is not a question of "doing" God's will, as though we need to produce or fabricate it. This third petition expresses the divine ambition for us to accomplish his will, to glorify him and participate in his reign. It reminds us that the will of God is the decisive criteria for cooperating with the sanctification of his name and the coming of his kingdom. Let us be attentive, however, not to "moralize" God's will. Romano Guardini remarks insightfully on this:

> We might perhaps be tempted to think that what is meant here is the "moral law" or our "duty" . . . But who would dream of praying, "May the moral law be fulfilled" or "May duty be done"? "The will of God" includes the moral law, for it enjoins upon human freedom the highest order, binding upon every conscience. But it is more than that—especially if we take the word in the particular abstract sense it has acquired in the modern age. The will of God is something infinite—a totality. It is something profound, near, living, which concerns us vitally and affects our being to its inmost depths. God's will is his holy intention for the world and for us. It is his eternal counsel, the fruit of his wisdom, the force of his stern decrees, the loving desire of his heart.[9]

Therefore, the meaning of the third petition of the *Our Father* is this: May your desire be lived out in our

---

9. Romano Guardini, *The Lord's Prayer*, trans. Isabel McHugh (Manchester, NH: Sophia Institute Press, 2014), pp. 4–5.

lives! This is God's ambition for us: to see us live out of his desire for us, that we might let his ambition be fully realized in our lives.

The Gift of Knowledge and Those Who Mourn

According to St. Augustine and St. Thomas, this petition calls upon the gift of knowledge (or "discernment").[10] The Holy Spirit does not only produce the gifts of fear and piety in us, which bring about a delicate love for God, but he makes us wise, teaching us to do the Father's will rather than our own.

To illustrate this, St. Thomas Aquinas uses the image of a patient who is willing to accept a painful remedy, because he trusts the doctor's opinion:

> Take the case of a sick man, who wishes for something from a physician. He does not wish this absolutely, but according to the physician's will. If he wished for it only according to his own will, he would be a fool. So we ought to ask nothing from God but those things which may be according to his will; that is to say, we ought to ask that his will may be fulfilled in us. For then man's heart is right when it is heartily one with the will of God.[11]

---

10. Aquinas, *The Lord's Prayer*, no. 10, p. 50.

11. Aquinas, *The Lord's Prayer*, no. 10, pp. 51–52.

When the way isn't easy, we must really trust in order to accept that God's will is superior to our own. This discernment is often made in tears. This is why St. Thomas adds, "By this petition we come to the beatitude of the mourners, of whom our Lord says: 'Blessed are those who mourn, for they shall be comforted'" (Mt 5:4).[12] Here we might think of Peter's tears when he encountered Jesus' loving gaze after having denied him. Suddenly he understood both the depth of his sin and the infinite tenderness of God for him. His heart of stone was transformed into a heart of flesh; water sprang forth from the rock. This is God's ambition for us: to transform our hearts of stone into hearts of flesh, that he might write his law on our hearts and that we might finally carry out his will.[13]

"Blessed are those who mourn, for they shall be comforted" (Mt 5:4). Our tears of discernment are only momentary, because God's consolation will follow. We must follow St. Peter's example, and weep for our denials so that we might be consoled by the risen Christ himself.[14] But the opposite is also true: when the Lord sends us his Spirit, the Comforter, how many are the

12. Aquinas, *The Lord's Prayer*, no. 12, p. 61.

13. See Ez 36:26 and Jer 31:33.

14. See Jn 21:15–19.

tears! They appear almost every day in the spiritual journal of St. Ignatius of Loyola, whose spirit of discernment is well known. Sometimes he writes, simply: "Tears before Mass, and many during it."[15]

4. "Give Us This Day Our Daily Bread"

(Living the Gift of Fortitude)

Meaning of the Fourth Petition

With the fourth petition, we go from "thy" to "us." We can certainly say "I" when we pray, but if Jesus taught us to say "us," it is to help us understand that the "I" of a Christian is also always an "us." The Christian "I" includes both the individual and the whole Church. We pray in our own name, and in the name of all. Every Christian participates in an "I" that is greater than their own, that of the entire Church.

The fourth petition of the *Our Father* is the prayer of petition *par excellence*, because it is a request for a gift. When we say, "give us," we are trusting in Divine Providence. God's ambition for us is so great, too great for us, that we can only attain it through him alone. This is why we ask him to give us what he expects of

15. See Ignatius of Loyola, *The Spiritual Diary of St. Ignatius of Loyola*, trans. William Young, S.J. (Woodstock, MD: Woodstock College Press, 1958), April 5, 1544.

us. As St. Augustine said, "Give what you command, and command what you will."[16] This is a prayer of trust, like that of a little child who asks his father for what he needs: "Give!"

In this way Jesus teaches us to ask the Father for what we need, to lead us into the spirit of childhood. What we need most is "bread," a word which here symbolizes every necessity. The word bread in Hebrew (*lechem*) does not only refer to what we call bread, but to everything that we eat. For example, in the book of Daniel when it is said that Balthasar the king "made a great feast," the word *lechem* is used. Clearly, we don't translate it as he "made a great bread" (Dn 5:1). In the general sense, bread is all food, all feasts, and by extension the symbol of all our needs.

However, we should note that, in this petition, the bread Jesus teaches us to ask for is qualified in a mysterious way. In Greek, we find a rare word here, almost unique, that we cannot translate perfectly: *epiousion*, "the bread of ours, the *epiouson*, given to us." We traditionally translate this word as "daily," and so we say, "give us this day our daily bread." But this does not exactly express the meaning of the Greek *epiousion*,

---

16. Augustine: *Da quod iubes et iube quod vis* (Confessions, 10, 29, 40; 31, 45; 37, 60).

which is made up of *epi* (on, above) and *ousia* (what one has, their property, substance). This is why St. Jerome tried to express this term through the Latin *supersubtantialis*, which we might translate as "super-essential" or "super-substantial." We must admit this remains mysterious, which is why the church fathers often understood this fourth petition as a direct allusion to the Eucharistic bread, which nourishes our supernatural life.

In this petition, we address God, asking him to give us what we need to accomplish his ambition and ours. If he wants us to do his will, he must also provide us with the necessary means, both supernatural (the Eucharist) and temporal (all other necessities). Fundamentally, we ask for the strength to accomplish our mission. This is why St. Augustine and St. Thomas connect this petition to the gift of fortitude.

The Gift of Fortitude and Hunger for Righteousness

This fourth petition complements the one before it. It is not enough to receive the gift of knowledge and discern God's will; we must then have the courage to accomplish it. One of the collects of the Mass summarizes this complementarity: "Lord, give us the grace to see what must be done (gift of knowledge) and the courage to accomplish it (gift of fortitude)." The gift of knowledge allows us to see what we need to do, but we must also receive the gift of fortitude so we can do what we have seen. We need this strength from above so that we don't lose courage, faced with the disparity between God's ambition for us and our limited capacity. It builds a foundation for our confidence and allows us to take on any struggles that might come our way, even if the fight seems disproportionate. Think of David, face to face with Goliath!

This is God's ambition for us: he wants to make us warriors. Isaiah says that the Lord "gives power to the faint, and to him who has no might he increases strength" (Is 40:29). Ezekiel had this very experience when the Holy Spirit entered him and set him firmly on his feet (See Ez 2:2). The Holy Spirit gives us fortitude, both so that we don't become weak from fear of lacking what we need, and to help us grow in confidence.

This is also probably why he teaches us to ask for our "daily" bread, and not our bread of tomorrow and the day after. We must learn to rely each day on the strength we receive from above through the Holy Spirit. This is how we can be satisfied and also remain in "hunger and thirst for righteousness." God gives us what we need while deepening our desire to go higher. As St. Thomas says: "From desire comes hunger, and from the hunger of the soul there comes the all-satisfying fulness of the life with God."[17] We must fight for justice, be hungry and thirsty for it, so that we can hope to be satisfied. But the opposite is also true. God's justice attracts us and deepens in us that hunger and thirst for a greater justice: the justice of heaven.

5. "Forgive Us Our Trespasses, as We Forgive Those Who Trespass Against Us"

(Living the Gift of Wisdom)

Meaning of the Fifth Petition

Petitions five through seven concern the obstacles which hinder us and threaten to reduce our noblest ambitions to nothing. There are three obstacles: the sin for which we ask forgiveness, the temptations we want to conquer, and the evil from which we want to be delivered.

Forgiveness of sins reminds us of the sad experience of being impacted by evil. We all find ourselves divided, even those who desire nothing but good. A moral dualism tears us apart. To one degree or another, we can all say like St. Paul, "I do not do the good I want, but the evil I do not want is what I do" (Rom 7:19). Some of us

---

17. Aquinas, *The Lord's Prayer*, no. 15, p. 74.

could even say, like Ovid, "I can see—and I approve—the better course, and yet I choose the worse."[18] Paul Ricœur expressed the depth of this drama in these few lines: "The 'fault' is an event with immense possibilities. At its outer limits it is a discovery of the infinite, an experience of the holy in reverse, of the holy in the demonic; it is sin in the strongest sense of the word."[19]

It is humbling to observe such irrationality in ourselves. Why is our will so fallible? When we think about it, moral wrongdoing is somewhat absurd. If we know something is bad, why do we choose it? Why is the mere possibility of evil so often transformed into action?

To understand how fallible man is, we must first address the question of original sin. Evil is only a possibility, but a possibility that attracts us all the same. This is because of an original wound we have inherited. As St. Thomas Aquinas says, "The inclination of reason would prevail in human nature in the state of integrity. But in corrupt nature the inclination of concupiscence

---

18. Ovid, *The Metamorphoses*, trans. Allen Mandelbaum (New York: Harcourt Brace, 1993), 7.20, p. 210. *Video meliora, proboque deteriora sequor.*

19. Paul Ricœur, *Freedom and Nature: The Voluntary and the Involuntary*, trans. Erazim V. Kohák (Evanston, IL: Northwestern University Press, 1966), p. 22.

prevails, because it is dominant in man."[20] This explains why it is inevitable that we sin, and this is why Jesus taught us to ask the Father to forgive our trespasses. Even taking original sin into account, his ambition remains that we be "holy and blameless before him" (Eph 1:4). But first we must be forgiven. He desires to forgive us and wants us to ask him for it.

The Gift of Counsel and the Merciful

According to St. Augustine and St. Thomas, this fifth petition is connected to the gift of counsel, for it is the Holy Spirit who encourages the sinner, by way of counsel, to ask God for the complete remission of his debts. Just as a doctor's advice helps a man who knows he is sick, the Holy Spirit's counsel will help when he knows he is a sinner. The man who has become spiritually sick through sin must ask the Holy Spirit for counsel to be healed. The Lord suggests not only that he ask the Father for forgiveness, but also that he offer pardon to those who have wounded him and carry out works of mercy toward others. This is why we see Daniel, in Scripture, give this wise advice to the sinister king Nebuchadnezzar: "Therefore, O king, let my counsel

20. Aquinas, *Summa Theologica*, 2-2.136.3.

be acceptable to you; break off your sins by practicing righteousness, and your iniquities by showing mercy to the oppressed" (Dn 4:27). St. Thomas comments: "The best counsel, then, against sin is almsgiving and mercy, and therefore the Holy Spirit teaches sinners to pray and to say 'Forgive us our debts.'"[21]

It is easy to connect this fifth petition to the beatitude: "Blessed are the merciful." We must show mercy toward others in order to receive mercy from God; at the same time, the more aware we are that we have received God's mercy, the more merciful we are with others. When we live as men and women who have been forgiven, we live a life of forgiving others.

But can we always forgive? Should we always? The *Catechism of the Catholic Church* answers this clearly:

> It is not in our power not to feel or to forget an offense; but the heart that offers itself to the Holy Spirit turns injury into compassion and purifies the memory in transforming the hurt into intercession. . . . Forgiveness is a high-point of Christian prayer; only hearts attuned to God's compassion can receive the gift of prayer.[22]

---

21. Aquinas, *The Lord's Prayer*, no. 16, p. 79.

22. *Catechism of the Catholic Church,* 2843–2844.

This is God's ambition for us: that our hearts be attuned to his infinite compassion. Jesus wanted to suffer on the Cross, asking his Father to forgive all: "Father, forgive them" (Lk 23:34). His incredible ambition for us is that we might also resemble him in this way.

6. "Lead Us Not Into Temptation"

(LIVING THE GIFT OF UNDERSTANDING)

Meaning of the Sixth Petition

If the petition for forgiveness of sins concerns the past, the petition to avoid temptation looks to the future. Guilt risks undermining our ambition to glorify God by convincing us we are not worthy, while the fear of falling can cause us to lose all daring. The Christian fighting spirit consists in living like St. Paul: "forgetting what lies behind and straining forward to what lies ahead, I press on toward the goal for the prize of the upward call of God in Christ Jesus" (Phil 3:13–14). This is only possible if God grants us not only forgiveness for the past, but also his assurance for the future. Thus, we have the sixth prayer of the *Our Father.*

To ask that we be not led "into temptation" does not exactly mean we ask not to be tempted at all; if Jesus himself was tempted, how could we not be tempted also?[23] Rather, this petition asks God to ensure we will not be conquered by temptation.

It is barely worth giving much consideration to our experience of temptation. We are stuck with it from the moment we reach the "age of reason," and doubtless even before that! There is an amusing little demonstration of this in a video called the "Marshmallow Test," based on a study led by psychologist Walter Mischel of Stanford University."[24] In it, several children are placed in front of a very appetizing marshmallow. Someone explains to the children that they can eat it, but if they wait until the person who brought them into the room comes back (about fifteen minutes later), they can have two marshmallows. They are filmed unknowingly, and it is amusing to watch them squirm in their seats—even if the whole thing seems a little cruel!

God never puts us to the test for fun like this.[25] On the contrary, he desires to free us from such situations. However, we cannot escape temptation because we are *de facto* engaged in a merciless combat between "the flesh and the Spirit." What a violent combat it can

---

23. See Mt 4:1–11.

24. See Walter Mischel, *The Marshmallow Test* (New York: Little, Brown & Co., 2014). For a video of the filmed experiment, see: vimeo.com/13390367.

25. See Jas 1:13.

sometimes be! As Homer said of Ulysses: "His heart growled within him . . . but he beat his breast and said, 'Heart, be still!'"[26]

We have already discussed this question of our interior division. Sometimes we feel as though we are two different people (or even "legion!")[27] We are able to see what is good and approve of it, and yet we let ourselves be led astray to what is worse. Temptation resides in this discrepancy between our knowledge and our desires. Drawing on Greek mythology, philosopher Donald Davidson discusses this as the *Medea Principle*, which he explains as: "what happens when Medea begs her own hand not to murder her children. Her hand, or the passion of revenge behind it, overcomes her will."[28]

So, we can know what is evil and be tempted to do it all the same. However, this discrepancy between our desire and our understanding is based on a sort of error or lie. If we are tempted to do evil, it is always because evil seems to us to be good, at least "here and now."

---

26. Homer, *The Odyssey*, trans. Samuel Butler, ed. Louise Loomis (Cabin John, MD: Wildside Press, 2021), ch. 20, p. 250.

27. See Mk 5:9.

28. Donald Davidson, "Paradoxes of Irrationality" in *The Essential Davidson* (Oxford: Oxford University Press, 2006), pp. 138–152. On the same subject, see his essay "How is Weakness of the Will Possible?," pp. 72–89.

We can certainly know it is evil in and of itself, and anticipate that later on we will repent of having chosen it, but in the moment it seems better than the idea of resisting. This is why, St. Thomas remarks, we might at certain times grieve for our sins and repent of them, while at other times we fall back into the same faults, accumulating reasons for future tears. Therefore, my conclusion is that temptation is always a sort of scam, based on a lie. This is why when we speak of the "devil" (which comes from the Greek *diabolos* or *dia-ballein*, which means literally "to set at variance" or "to divide"), or when we speak of the "temptor," or the "prince of lies," it all amounts to the same thing.

The Gift of Understanding and Purity of Heart

Since temptation always comes from a lie, St. Thomas connects the petition "Lead us not into temptation" to the gift of understanding. This gift helps us to affectively discern truth from falsehood, to the point of fleeing with horror from every form of lie: "He rules and guides us by the light of understanding, for by this he instructs us about the things that we ought to do."[29] David asked for this light which comes from the gift of

29. Aquinas, *The Lord's Prayer*, no. 18, p. 102.

understanding when he said, "Consider and answer me, O Lord my God; lighten my eyes, lest I sleep the sleep of death; lest my enemy say, 'I have prevailed over him'" (Ps 13:3–4).

When God gives you an idea, it's an inspiration. When the devil gives you an idea, it's a temptation! We must decide each day, with God's grace, which idea will be the basis for our actions and serve our ambition. When we refuse temptation, we keep our hearts from becoming mixed up, and so it is fitting to place the sixth petition of the *Our Father* in parallel with the sixth beatitude: "Blessed are the pure in heart, for they shall see God." We must have a pure heart to see God, and inversely, nothing purifies us more than the desire to contemplate him face to face. As St. John says, "we shall be like him, for we shall see him as he is" (1 Jn 3:2).

7. "But Deliver Us From Evil"

(Living the Gift of Wisdom)

Meaning of the Seventh Petition

In petitions five and six, we ask the Father to be forgiven of our sins and to avoid temptation. In the final petition, we implore him for total liberation from evil and the devil. Forgiveness of sins concerns the past, temptation concerns the future, and deliverance from evil concerns the present. This is a sort of synthesis of the three dimensions of spiritual combat present in our temporal existence. The evil that we have done causes us guilt, the evil we might do causes us fear, and the evil that assails us causes alienation.

But what is evil? Let's make it simple and say that evil is the lack of good. And since the absolute good is God, we might say that absolute evil is the lack of God. The final petition of the *Our Father* therefore moves us to ask that we might never be deprived of God, or that we might come back to him quickly if we have drifted away. "Restore us, O God; let thy face shine, that we may be saved!" (Ps 80:3).

We must note that the Greek word used here for evil (*ponêros*) can also be translated as "the devil." The meaning of the final petition therefore is both general ("deliver us from evil in all its forms") and specific ("deliver us from the evil one," meaning Satan). This translation follows the two preceding petitions: after asking for forgiveness of our sins and victory over temptation, we ask to be liberated from the one who, through temptation, leads us into sin. In fact, this is Jesus' explicit request for us in his great and final prayer in Chapter seventeen of St. John's Gospel: "Father . . . I do not pray that thou shouldst take them out of the world, but that thou shouldst keep them from the evil one" (Jn 17:1,15).

Deliverance from evil in general, and the devil in particular, expresses God's ultimate ambition for us: to see us free! God wants us to be free for him, no longer shackled by sin, guilt, and despair. When the Hebrew people were slaves in Egypt, they lost their great ambitions. They no longer imagined escaping Pharaoh's power; they had come to terms with it. Their wildest dreams were only to hope for an easing of their burden. Thankfully, God had greater plans for them: he desired their freedom!

The Gift of Wisdom and the Peacemakers

In his commentary on the *Our Father*, St. Thomas parallels this petition for deliverance with the gift of wisdom. His explanation is difficult to understand and even seems a little far-fetched, but it is interesting, nonetheless. According to him, the divine way of delivering man from evil is to transform the evil into good, and this is "a proof of the greatest wisdom. It is the part of a wise man to make evils lead to good."[30] To understand St. Thomas' assertion, we need to know there is a connection between wisdom and order, just

30. Aquinas, *The Lord's Prayer*, no. 19, p. 111.

as there is a connection between madness and disorder. According to the adage of the Ancients: "the wise man should give orders."[31] As God is eminently wise, he has not only set everything "by measure and number and weight" (Wis 11:20), but he re-establishes order in the world, in the very place where the devil introduced chaos. How does he do this?

St. Thomas' suggested response is barely exciting at a first reading, but it is quite profound (if not unfathomable) when we ponder it:

> God frees man from evils and tribulations by changing them into blessings. . . . It is the part of a wise man to make evils lead to good, and he does this by the patience with which he bears his trials. Now other virtues are exercised about good; but patience is exercised about evils. Patience therefore is only necessary in evils, that is in trials: "The learning of a man is known by patience; and his glory is to pass over wrongs." (Prv 19:11)[32]

This is why, according to St. Thomas, the Holy Spirit enables us to make this final petition to the Father, through the gift of wisdom.

---

31. Aristotle, *Metaphysics*, 982a17.

32. Aquinas, *The Lord's Prayer*, no. 19, p. 111.

St. Thomas adds that through this gift, we attain the beatitude of the peacemakers:

> For by patience, we have peace in sorrow, and by patience we have peace in joy. Well then may the peacemakers be called the children of God, for they are like God. As nothing can do injury to God, so neither prosperity nor adversity can injure the peaceful. Jesus says, "Blessed are the peacemakers, for they shall be called the children of God." (Mt 5:9)[33]

The peacemaker is a son of God in that he resembles him, for God is the "Prince of Peace." But the opposite is even more true: when God's peace pervades our hearts, through an inexpressible gift, everything in us becomes filial in regard to the Father. This is when we can truly say: "Our Father."

33. Aquinas, *The Lord's Prayer*, no. 19, p. 111.

10

Our Father Who Art in Heaven, Make a Heaven of the Earth

I WOULD NOW LIKE TO ADDRESS the *incipit* of the Lord's Prayer, "Our Father who art in heaven," as well as the conclusion of the first three petitions, "on earth as it is in heaven." In doing so, I will highlight the very essence of Christian ambition which is, in the end, to unite heaven and earth.

The language used here is symbolic, and no longer as familiar to us as it once was. It might therefore be useful to begin with a few words about the symbols of earth and heaven, and their biblical meaning.

We might think of the earth as an element (just like water, air, and fire), or as a space (the terrestrial globe, the world, habitable area, terrain, territory, and so on). In Greek mythology, the earth is personified and given the name of the goddess Gaia, the source of all. It is therefore considered sacred.

In the Bible, however, the earth lacks this same grandeur, understood more in reference to the dust from which man is made and to which he will return because of sin. We speak of the "*Holy* Land," but it is only holy because God's presence has sanctified it.[1] The earth is only fertile in the measure that it is turned toward heaven, awaiting the rain. When Jesus teaches us to ask that the Father's will be done on earth as in heaven, we are asking that our earth, our land, our environment, our world, be made fertile by God's presence. We express our ambition to see our world finally resemble that of "heaven."

But what do the symbolism of heaven and the heavens represent? What we call heaven or the heavens are the things related to what is above, which we can only see when we raise our eyes. This symbolically expresses the divine ambition which dwells in man's heart.

When we begin by invoking the Father who is "in heaven," we immediately raise our souls to the Most High. This is, in fact, the classic definition of prayer: raising the soul to God. Since God is Love, we might say that heaven symbolically refers to the definitive accomplishment of human existence through perfect

---

1. See Ex 3:5 (cited in Acts 7:33); Zec 2:12; 2 Mc 1:7; Wis 12:3; 2 Kgs 5:17.

love. Heaven, therefore, does not refer to a literal space, but rather to a way of being. Heaven is being united to God in perfect love.

We should add that, according to Origen, the phrase "on earth as it is in heaven" is connected to each of the first three petitions, and not just to the third one. For if God's name is sanctified among those who dwell in heaven, if God's reign is established in them, if God's will is done through them, all of these are "things which are lacking in us who are on earth, but they can be granted to us if we render ourselves worthy to obtain them from God, who hears all of these petitions."[2] We might, therefore, translate Jesus' prayer like this: "Our Father in heaven, may your name be sanctified, your kingdom come, and your will be done, all on earth as in heaven."[3]

Here, we have the principle of God's divine ambition for us: that we might already anticipate the glory of heaven here on earth, and that earth might be made to resemble heaven. When we pray the *Our Father*, we turn immediately toward heaven and recognize that all our ambition can only find efficacy through him.

---

2. Origen, "De la prière," in A. Hamman, *Le Pater expliqué par les Pères* (Paris: Éditions franciscaines, 1952), ch. 26, no. 2, p. 54. Our translation.

3. Jean Carmignac, *À l'écoute du Notre Père* (Paris: Éditions de Paris, 1969), p. 43. Our translation.

But here, we might raise an objection. Is this not idealism? Nietzsche accused Christianity of being a sort of "Platonism for the people."[4] This is where Zarathustra's anti-homily comes from: "I beseech you, my brothers, *remain faithful to the earth*, and do not believe those who speak to you of otherworldly hopes! Poison-mixers are they, whether they know it or not."[5] This is a poor understanding of God's ambition for us. He does not invite us to fulfil heavenly ideals here on earth, to send us flying toward the sun like Icarus of Greek mythology. He invites us, rather, to enter, here and now, into the very mystery of God and to live of his blessing. Our life can only become a holy land if it is divinized through heavenly action. We need God's grace for our lives to bear fruit, just as the earth is turned toward heaven, offering itself that it might drink of the springs of heavenly rain and live from the blessings sent from above. This does not prevent us from loving the earth and being faithful to it. On the contrary, it is necessary for Adam to work the earth (let us be wary of quietism), but he waits for heaven to send the rain.

---

4. Friedrich Nietzsche, preface to *Beyond Good and Evil*, p. 2.

5. Nietzsche, "Thus Spoke Zarathustra" in *The Portable Nietzsche*, trans. Walter Kaufman (New York: Penguin Books, 1976), first part, 3, p. 125.

CONCLUSION

"His ambitions for us are so great!"[1]

—St. Thérèse of Lisieux

THE TRUE MEASURE of Christian ambition is God's ambition for us. Nothing less. God wants us to aim wider, further, higher, deeper.

> [I pray that you] may have power to comprehend with all the saints what is the breadth and length and height and depth, and to know the love of Christ which surpasses knowledge, that you may be filled with all the fulness of God. (Eph 3:17–19)

As we conclude, let us look at these four dimensions St. Paul speaks of (breadth, height, length, and depth), and consider them as an expression of the "geometry of divine ambition," or its "cubic measure."

1. Thérèse of Lisieux, "Letter 57," *Œuvres Complètes* (Paris: Cerf-DDB, 1997), p. 350. Our translation.

1. Broader

"Its measure is . . . broader than the sea."

—JOB 11:9

St. Paul begins with the "latitude" of this mystery. "Breadth" speaks particularly to the expanse of divine love, which surpasses all things and extends even to its enemies. As the psalmist says: "Thy commandment is exceedingly broad" (Ps 119:96). This is the first dimension of divine ambition that we should become aware of. God's love is broad. It extends to all creatures, and particularly to all of humanity, without any exception. He wants us to resemble him in this way. God wants our wisdom and our love to be wider; he wants our prayer and our actions to encompass the whole world.

This requires us to truly become aware of the breadth of the Lord's merciful love, which reaches to every creature and to every dimension of our life. God's love does not only surround the little island of "me" that we so cherish; it is like an ocean which reaches to every beach in the world. His ambition is for everyone: "[God] desires all men to be saved and to come to the knowledge of the truth" (1 Tm 2:4). This is also what St. John prophecies in his book of Revelation: "I looked, and behold, a great multitude which no man could number, from every nation, from all tribes and peoples and tongues . . ." (Rv 7:9–10).

This immense multitude, made up of all sorts of differences, is also in us. Our personal lives are so full of variety! They are made up of beautiful things, good actions—and a heap of less impressive things. How good it is to consider that the divine ocean can cover all of it with love and forgiveness.

None of our occupations or preoccupations escape him. They say that Alexander the Great knew the name of each of his soldiers! That's not bad, but he certainly didn't know each of their worries. Their interior life was a mystery to him, whereas God knows ours perfectly.

The more we become aware of the infinite breadth of God's love, the more we enlarge our heart and our spirit, just as Isaiah says: "Enlarge the place of your tent. (Is 54:2)" This is an invitation to think, to love, to receive and to live more broadly. St. Augustine expresses this well:

> For just as, if you would fill a bag, and know how great the thing is that shall be given, you stretch the opening of the sack or the skin, or what else it be; you know how much you would put in, and see that the bag is narrow; by stretching you make it

> capable of holding more: so God, by deferring our hope, stretches our desire; by the desiring, stretches the mind; by stretching, makes it more capacious . . . let us stretch ourselves unto him, that when he come, he may fill us.[2]

2. Longer

"*Its measure is longer than the earth.*"

—JOB 11:9

After the latitude of God's ambition, St. Paul refers to its longitude. If breadth refers to the expanse of divine ambition, length speaks more to its duration, its eternity. This begins for us here on earth, at the moment of our conception, and will be perfectly accomplished in glory, but in God there is no beginning or end. His love is "from everlasting to everlasting" (Ps 103:17). His plans for us extend from age to age. Being aware of this allows us to relativize our small ambitions and our failures of the moment, allowing us to enter into something greater than we can imagine: God's eternal design for us. Our ambition is part of an infinitely greater temporality.

2. Augustine, "Homily Four on the First Epistle of John," no. 6.

Think of this: if God looked at us for even several short minutes, it would be a great honor for us. But in reality he has been looking at us forever, into eternity, because his love is eternal. As he himself said to the prophet Jeremiah: "I have loved you with an everlasting love" (Jer 31:3). This means that his love for us has no beginning, nor end, nor interruption:

1. God's love for us did not start at the beginning of our existence, nor when our parents or grandparents began to exist. It has preceded us for all of time.
2. God's love for us will never cease, for God does not change; he "is the same yesterday and today and forever" (Heb 13:8).
3. Since his love does not cease, neither does it diminish. Nor is it interrupted. God is not sporadic with his love! Even our most serious sins cannot put his love on pause, much less switch it off. God has no "Intermittences of the Heart" (Proust).

Living in God's ambition for us requires that we enter into a plan of love that is much greater than we can envision. When we love, our perspective is not that of death, but of eternity. When we search for truth, we are only beginning a journey here on earth that will end in the brilliant light of glory. We are simply preparing in time for the coming of the Eternal.

3. Higher

"*It is higher than heaven—*
what can you do?"
—JOB 11:8

After latitude and longitude comes the height. The Bible often sings of God's height: "The Lord is high above all nations, and his glory above the heavens" (Ps 113:4). This dimension suggests the idea of elevation. It speaks of God's desire to see us incline ourselves toward the things of heaven, loving him for himself and not simply for the sake of a few worldly benefits. Christ's Ascension is an example of this. Raised higher than the angels, he sits at the right hand of the Father and prepares a place for us "in heaven" (See Jn 14:1–3).

The height to which we are called is the very height of God "in heaven," and this is why he calls us to live by going from height to height: "Friend, go up higher" (Lk 14:10).

This is what Alexander Solzhenitsyn proclaimed at the end of his famous speech given at Harvard in 1978, entitled "A World Split Apart."

> "If the world has not approached its end, it has reached a major watershed in history . . . It will demand from us a spiritual blaze; we shall have to rise to a new height of vision, to a new level of life. . . . No one on earth has any other way left but—upward."[3]

4. Deeper

"*It is . . . deeper than Sheol—*
what can you know?"

—Job 11:8

After latitude, longitude, and height, we come to the depth of divine ambition for us. St. Paul uses the Greek word *bathos*, which refers to the depth of the ocean, the unfathomable abyss. It signifies the incomprehensibility of divine wisdom, whose origin we cannot reach. "The height of heaven, the breadth of the earth, the abyss, and wisdom—who can search them out?" asks Ben Sirach (Sir 1:3). We should not understand "abyss" to mean "some great unknown thing." God's ambition for us is not that we sink into some obscure and

3. Alexander Solzhenitsyn, *A World Split Apart* (New York: Harper Collins, 1978).

irrational chasm. On the contrary, it calls us to dive ever more into his mystery of love and light. The more we ponder God's infinity, the more we will experience the ecstasy of St. Paul: "O the depth of the riches and wisdom and knowledge of God! How unsearchable are his judgements and how inscrutable his ways!" (Rom 11:33).

The abyss of God's mystery appears to us in the greatest simplicity and silence. It is no longer a question of endless reasoning, but of simply being present to the one who is infinitely present.